From the Library of:
Patricia Gibbons
5533 Folkstone Drive
Troy, MI 48085

QUIET TALKS

ABOUT

The Healing Christ

By
S. D. GORDON
Author of "Quiet Talks on Power,"
"Quiet Talks on Prayer" etc.

New York   Chicago
Fleming   H.   Revell   Company
London   and   Edinburgh

Copyright, 1924, by
FLEMING H. REVELL COMPANY

Printed in the United States of America

New York: 158 Fifth Avenue
Chicago: 17 North Wabash Ave.
London: 21 Paternoster Square
Edinburgh: 75 Princes Street

Printing Statement:

Due to the very old age and scarcity of this book, many of the pages may be hard to read due to the blurring of the original text, possible missing pages, missing text and other issues beyond our control.

Because this is such an important and rare work, we believe it is best to reproduce this book regardless of its original condition.

Thank you for your understanding.

Some Principles of Healing

As Taught in God's Word, Directly and Indirectly

1. It is God's first will that men be pure in heart, clear in mind, strong in purpose, gentle and content in spirit, poised in judgment, happy in circumstances, and strong and well in body.
2. God does not send disease. It comes through some disobedience of the natural laws of the body, conscious or unconscious, though rarely traceable in full. It may come from the Devil, *or,* because of the break of sin affecting all life. But *always through* that open door of disobedience to the laws of the body.
3. Christ heals men's bodies to-day by His own direct supernatural touch, sometimes through the physician and the use of means, sometimes without means, sometimes when means are confessedly powerless, and sometimes overcoming the unwise use of means. The Holy Spirit's leading is the touchstone.
4. In healing Christ is always reaching in for the far greater thing, the healing of the spirit, the life.
5. There is sometimes a waiting time, after the conditions are met, before the full healing

comes. There is a disciplinary side in bodily suffering, but the healing comes as quickly as the lesson is learned.
6. The Devil heals men's bodies, within sharply defined limits, under disguise, that he may get and tighten his hold on man. He bitterly opposes healing through Christ's supernatural touch. This is particularly true regarding those that have the gift of leadership.
7. The conditions for Christ's healing are the same as for being saved. Trust Him fully as your Saviour and Master. Then go to Him for whatever you need, always seeking the Holy Spirit's guidance.

CONTENTS

	PREFACE	11
I.	THE CHRIST HEALING	15

Doing impossible things — Why the crowds came — Twenty-four healing miracles—Mostly incurable—List of diseases treated—Extent of power—Effect on crowds—Why Christ healed—"I forgot."

II.	IS IT CHRIST'S WILL TO HEAL OUR BODIES TO-DAY?	24

The need—Medical science—Physicians and drugs—Eden—Job at the front door—Healing-teaching trail—Acts the Church Book—Eight instances—Ephesus center—Corinth center—Some not healed—The Epistles—Twofold aim—Immunity from death—"Paralysis, heart disease."

III.	DOES GOD SEND SICKNESS AND DISEASE?	43

A religion of power—Christ's incidental by-products — Christianity's distinctive trait—Foreign mission objective—Common impression about origin of disease—The teaching of the Book—The Job story—Healing threefold—John Ruskin's copper kettle—An English woman in Algiers.

IV.	How Does Christ Heal? The Conditions: The Method: The Use of Means	63

Natural and Supernatural—Twofold objective in healing—The "How" of conditions—Act, purpose, habit, attitude—The "How" of method—A Christian physician—Seven ways healing comes—Four natural, two supernatural—Use of Means—Pope Leo—Homely touches—A poultice of figs—"Faith Street"—Two cancer cases—Fever.

V.	How Far May Christ's Healing Be Expected? Christ's Giving and Man's Taking . . .	95

Wide range of disease—Healed but limping—Eye-glasses—Teeth—Dentistry—Extent of Christ's healing—And in the Acts—The answer twofold—Ask Christ—"Take"—Taking three-sided—How to take—Rheumatoid arthritis—A club-foot.

VI.	The Human Side of Healing and Health	113

The break in the rhythm—The remarkable Hebrew health trail—Adam-in-Eden model—True Christian life—Effect of mental attitude on body—Slavish fear—Ninety per cent. of diseases above the ears—The condemned murderer—Poisoned milk—Graying hair stopped—A surprising prescription—Obedience to laws of body—Seven items—Nine common sins.

Contents

VII. GOD'S SCHOOL OF SUFFERING: CAN WE HASTEN GRADUATION DAY? . 152
Experience as teacher—Fees—Saintly stubbornness—Weak strong points—The Schoolmaster—The Job story—Six chapters — The twofold purpose — Paul's thorn—The threefold answer—The continuous healing touch on Paul—Jacob's limp—A threefold crisis—Graduation Day—"Under the bed."

VIII. THE DEVIL'S HEALING: IMITATIONS AND COUNTERFEITS . . . 193
The Devil's trail—Two sources of supernatural power—The Devil's miracles—Egypt—Sharp limitations—The coming crisis—The Devil's healings to-day—A double healing in Berlin—Spirit discernment—How gotten.

Preface

CHRIST will meet every need of a man's life. And He will meet it eagerly and to the full.

If we don't have all we need the trouble isn't with the Hand that gives but the hand that takes.

No man's hand has ever yet reached up to take as much as the Pierced Hand is reaching down to give.

But giving is a fine art, so as not to hurt in trying to help. And the taking needs skill, too, though the simplest may take all he needs. Skill in taking is chiefly skill of the heart.

Teaching is rare. Matured rounded-out teaching is yet more rare. And the chief need to-day, in the bustle and dust of much stirring about, is teaching, simple, clear, full, poised teaching.

Healing is one of the tangled subjects. Two others keep it close company, so far as being tangled is concerned, namely, holiness, and the return of Christ.

It is easy to get warped unmatured partial statements, quite honestly made, on these subjects.

The direct preparation of this little book has taken eleven years, the indirect runs further back. I didn't set out to write a book.

I felt the need of getting my own feet on a

difficult bit of pavement. I read and watched and prayed to understand for myself.

And now the substance of it is given to others, with a prayer that it may, possibly, help them a little as it has helped me.

Two books have been constantly studied, the Book of God, and the Book of Life. These two go together.

The Book of God is written out of life, under the Holy Spirit's touch and control. The Book of Life is still being written.

It takes a simple skill of habitual reading to understand the first. It takes a careful trained reading habit to read understandingly the second.

The Book of God is the teaching book, written out of human experience, and full of illustrations out of life.

The Book of Life is the illustration book. There are countless illustrations on every hand of all the teachings of the other book.

One wants to read both. They fit together. And the conditions for understanding both are the same, a bent will, an open mind, a prayerful spirit, a keenly observing eye, and the constant practised reading.

So there comes the discernment of our Father's purposes and plans, *and* of how things are working out in actual life.

The instances of healing given here are all known to me personally, with four exceptions. In each case I took pains to get the exact facts of what actually took place. Else, of course, I would not tell these incidents in this open positive way. The facts are clear. These are a few out of the many.

The four exceptions are, the two from my personal friend, Mr. James Moore Hickson of London, the one from my German deaconess friend of Berlin, and the one from a Texas friend. These four instances are known personally to these friends, who told me.

And I have full confidence, not merely in their sincerity, but what is more important here because not so common, in their trained accuracy in observation of actual facts, and in their careful detailed description of what they saw and know.

And so, after these years of study, the little messenger is sent out in Christ's name. And the one conscious purpose is that it may help some to reach up and *take* all the Pierced Hand is now reaching down to *give*.

I
THE CHRIST HEALING

It is God's first will for every man, everywhere, that he shall be pure in heart, straight in life, strong in purpose, clear and open in mind, well-balanced in judgment, gentle in contact with others, at peace within, happy in circumstances, and strong and well in his body.

Humanly Impossible.

CHRIST did impossible things, when He was down here. That is, they were impossible to others. He did them.

They were things that needed to be done. Men were helped by them. The tug of living was eased, and more. It took power to do them.

It took a power more than the natural power men were familiar with. Others didn't do them. They couldn't. They didn't have the power. Christ had the power needed. He did them. He did impossible things.

Christ taught. He is commonly accepted as the race's greatest teacher. Then there was more. He lived what He taught. He lived it first before He taught it.

He lived it far more than even He could teach it. There was always a reserve of teaching actually lived back of the teaching taught. But there was more than teaching. Christ did things.

He had ideals. His ideals have clean out-idealed the ideals of all others. But there was more than ideals. He brought things to pass in actual life. Men saw and felt and experienced things through His touch, things they needed and needed sorely, but didn't have till He did them.

The distinctive thing about Christ, of course, is that He died. He died as none other did, nor could, nor can. The most outstanding thing about His life is the end of it. The knot on the end of the thread of His life, that gathered it all up in one, is His death.

But apart from that, the outstanding thing is that Christ did impossible things. Men admire and worship the man who can do outstanding things, actually bring them to pass. Christ did outstanding things.

He fed the hungry thousands with a few scanty loaves. How they'd like to have Him in some parts of Europe just now, if His activities could be restricted within desired limits.

He stilled that sudden Galilean storm that blanched the bronzed cheeks of those hardened sailors, stilled it with a word; and stilled it into a great calm.

He helped Peter pay his taxes, in a very unusual way. That has a very practical sound to-day. He robbed the ever-yawning grave of its hopeless victims.

Of all things Christ did one stands out biggest. He healed men's bodies of sickness and disease. The world was sick when Christ was here. There was no science of bodily healing.

There was a natural healing. The Jews have

been famous through the centuries for their rare skill in healing through simple remedies. But, characteristically, dominantly, the race was sick. Christ healed men's bodies.

This was the thing that first drew the crowds in notable numbers. That fact itself tells how acute things were in this regard. The need was so sore, and so general, that once the word went out, it spread like a blessed wild-fire.

And the crowds came from everywhere, and they came a-crowding so thick as to affect seriously His movements.

Hopeless Incurables.

There are thirty-three instances given of miracles done by Christ. And twenty-eight of them have to do with the body. Twenty-four of them were miracles of healing (including now the three cases of death). Four others have to do with supplying bodily needs.

There are sixteen summaries given of His various activities, including bodily healing. If one run over these summaries the first-flush, rough impression comes that the total of those healed probably ran into some several thousands. People came in throngs. They came from all the surrounding countries, as far away as Tyre and the Upper Mediterranean.

There are twenty-four individual instances of healing, given in the four Gospels. These become of intense interest for what they tell of Christ's healing ministry. Of the twenty-four two would be classed as acute cases.

The other twenty-two are all chronic cases, incurables, extreme hopeless incorrigibles. Six (possibly eight) were demon-possessed, reckoned quite incurable. Three were actually dead. The thirteen others were distinctly hopeless incurables.

The healing power went to the last degree of human need. The humanly impossible yielded to Christ's touch every time. There were no exceptions so far as the soreness of the need was concerned.

The story told is quite explicit on this point. Here is the list of diseases specifically named,— epilepsy, dropsy, deaf and dumb, palsy or paralysis, chronic hemorrhage, demon-possession, leprosy, withered hand (*i. e.*, paralysis), blind, infirmities (possibly paralysis), restoration of ear cut off, and even the dead, three times named in three distinct stages.

There is one outstanding passage that touches the extreme of need which Christ's healing covered. Matthew says "There came unto Him great multitudes, having with them the lame, blind, dumb, *maimed,* and many others, and cast them down at His feet; and He healed them."[1] It is a significant passage.

It was clearly an unusual crowd of helpless incurables, brought by their kinsfolk and friends and neighbours. What a sight!

That word "maimed" catches one's eye. It occurs twice. The word underneath has two meanings, crooked is one, and *mutilated* the

[1] Matthew 15:30.

other. Its use in Mark 9:43 clearly means a limb quite gone.

The word under "lame" here is also used in the Mark passage for a limb cut off. The meaning intended here is quite clear. The healing went to the extent of restoring a lost portion of the body, a limb or an arm or some other part.

The extent of healing as regards the need is made quite clear, and is as sweeping as clear. There were no exceptions so far as need went.

A Bubbling-over Power at Work.

The extent of Christ's power to heal is put in as sweeping language. His power always covered fully the man's need, whatever that chanced to be. There was simply no limit. His healing met every need, and met it fully. It could not have been greater. Three words can be used, Christ healed instantly, perfectly, and permanently.

There is one exception frankly spoken of. Once, the healing went through two stages. First the man saw men "as trees walking," then "all things clearly." The interval of time involved was plainly so brief that, I think likely, the man himself would have gladly used the word "instantly."

Again that outstanding passage comes in. Its language could not be more graphic and adequate, and yet simple and brief. Matthew says "The multitudes wondered when they saw the dumb speaking, the maimed whole, and the lame walking, and the blind seeing."[1]

The extent of the power at work is as striking as the sweep of disease covered. There's a bubbling-over exuberance, an overflowing abundance. The crowds came to know that if they would "only touch the border of His garment" they would know the healing power in their body.

It says "power came forth from Him," as though it breathed out of His very presence. The ease of action, the abundance of power, and the frequency and extent of Christ's healing power stand in striking contrast to the Old Testament miracles.

And the effect on the crowds itself revealed the touch of God. "They *glorified*" God. There was an exuberant singing of praise to such a God. Even the curious crowds that came seeking sensation found a sort that sent them away with a hush in their hearts, and praises to God on their lips.

And, it is striking to note, that Christ gave this power to His disciples, unschooled and undisciplined as they were, yet devoted to Him.

Repeatedly they were sent out into the villages and country districts. And they returned with ringing voices and shining faces, telling of the power that had attended their activity. And usually special emphasis is laid on healing, and on the casting out of evil spirits.

[1] Matthew 15: 31.

The Christ Healing

Why Did Christ Heal?

It becomes of intense interest to note why Christ healed, so far as the Gospel record goes. It is never intimated that He did it to let people know that He could. He never used power simply to let men see He had it.

It is never suggested that He did mighty works to prove His distinctive personality, who He was. This simply is not referred to. Incidentally it is made clear that He did have the exceptional power, and that He was the Son of God in the distinctive sense that was true of no other.

Even when John, in the dark of the prison cell, puzzled to know why Christ didn't fill out the official side of the Messiah's task, as well as the personal side, even to him Christ simply points out what was being done as evidence that the old prophetic picture was being lived out.

He comforts the lone prison vigil with word that John had been true. And that there was a waiting time ahead for both of them.

No, Christ healed men because He couldn't help it. Their sore need, so sore, tugged desperately at His heart. He healed men because they needed healing. This stands out first and foremost. There is more, a big more, but in the Gospel narratives it is always incidental.

It is true, broadly, as a principle, that miracles, the supernatural, came into action, throughout Scripture, to meet some emergency. But, when it comes to the immediate reason why Christ healed, as the narrative runs, it was to meet the personal need of suffering men and women.

There is a strong, tender word constantly on His lips, and spoken of Himself, "compassion." It means to have the heart tenderly drawn out by need. It really means to suffer in heart because of the suffering of others.

This gives the "why" of Christ's healing. One key-passage may be given as an index to the others, "He had compassion on them, *and* healed their sick."[1]

He healed because He couldn't help it. He *could* heal, and He couldn't help healing, with such suffering before His eyes. His heart must answer to such needs. The healing is a window into Christ's heart. And Christ Himself is the open window into the Father's heart.

One afternoon late a gentle-faced woman came at the close of the meeting and asked abruptly, "Does God answer prayer?" She had a thoughtful face, and looked like one well cared for.

I didn't say "yes." A mere yes seemed too tame with that tense face, and those suffering eyes. I merely said "Sit down a moment."

And with a bit of prayer for guidance, I said, " Has He ever answered a prayer for you? just once?" For, you remember, one fact establishes a law of action.

Instantly a startled look came into her eye. And in a low hushed voice she said, "Oh! I

---

[1] Matthew 14:14. See also 15:32, 20:34, 9:36 with 10:1. Mark 1:41, 6:34, 8:2, Luke 7:13-15.

forgot." Then she told in a few words of when her daughter, years before, a child of ten or so then, had been critically ill. And the physician had said that the knife must be used.

Her mother heart drew back from having a surgeon's knife cut into that precious little body. Could she have a little time to think about that, she had asked. Yes, there was no immediate pressure, was the reply.

That night she had retired for sleep. She spent much more time than usual on her knees. She didn't ask for healing. She had not been taught that she might.

She simply poured out her heart. God was a father. He was so good. It troubled her so sorely to have the knife used. Just a cry out of her heart, a yearning cry, inarticulate as to the how.

Then she slept quietly. The morning came, and the physician. And after the examination a puzzled look came into his eyes.

And he said quietly, "I don't just understand this; but a distinct change has come in your daughter's condition. I won't need to use the knife. She will get well without it." And she did.

And the woman said with a changed voice, "I forgot." Her own experience answered her tense question.

Is it not a winsome bit out of life? Christ has not changed. His power is at our fingertips now. No need need go unsupplied, if He may have His way.

II

IS IT CHRIST'S WILL TO HEAL OUR BODIES TO-DAY?

It is God's first will that men should be pure in heart, gripped by a nobly strong purpose, poised in our understanding of things, humanly gentle in our personal contacts, at sweet peace within, content in circumstances, and healthy and hearty in our bodies.

The World is Sick.

Is it Christ's will to heal our bodies of sickness and disease and weakness to-day? He can, of course. He has the power.

Is He willing to do it? Does He think it wise to? Is it part of His plan for us at the present time?

There is need enough surely, so far as that goes. And surely that must go far with God. The race is sick to-day.

Oh! there is more health than disease, more strength than weakness, more life than death. This is true. Yet the race is sick and diseased. That fact pushes its ugly self in at every turn.

And there is a science of bodily healing to-day. It is quite modern. It was non-existent up until recent decades. It is a real science, properly so called.

It is based on actual knowledge of the human body, and of substances found in nature, and of their action on the body.

It is based upon a vast accumulation of experience, and of skill. It is accurately called a science, really a rare combination of science and of art, acquired skill in action.

Of course, there are poor preachers, and poor lawyers, and poor physicians. The personal equation affects things enormously here, as everywhere.

There is confessedly a vast amount of guesswork and of experimenting, at human expense of pain and suffering, and worse. Yet there is a real science of healing.

There is a not-good professional pride here, as in all professional circles. And, say it very gently, that certainly doesn't help any one. And there is an unhappy tendency, sharply marked and growing, toward a commercialism in all the noble professions.

Yet the fact stands out blessedly that there is a science of bodily healing. And its gracious ministrations among men, through the years, in actual healing, and in relieving, is clear beyond words to describe or imagination to picture.

It's a striking fact that some of the most prominent leaders in this notable science have shown certain distinct tendencies, away from drugs and the knife, and toward advice about the intelligent care of the body.

A long list might be given of quotations from the most eminent of physicians, in highest position, in England and America and the Continent, against the use of drugs, and concerning the actual injuries inflicted by guesswork and experiment. These quotations magnify the place of nature in healing, through means, aside from remedies, and often overcoming the drugs given.

There is an emphasis by these leaders on intelligence in selection of foods, a wise obedience to bodily laws, and on the distinct bearing of the mental and spirit mood and attitude on bodily conditions.

And, it should be noted with strong emphasis, that, quite apart from any direct action on God's part, one's mental attitude has incalculable influence on the body. It affects the bodily conditions greatly at all times, and in disease and times of crisis it is pretty apt to be the decisive factor.

Fear, the fear that's afraid, opens the door to disease. It actually creates poisons in one's body. A simple heart-trust in God, and His goodness, with the confident atmosphere that belongs with it, actually creates healthy conditions in the body. I am not speaking now of the numerous imaginary ills, but of actual physical conditions.

Yet, notwithstanding the science of healing, the fact stands out at every corner, pathetically, tragically, that the world is sick, bodily ill. A recent article in a prominent daily, based on carefully compiled statistics, gathered through a period of years, estimated that between two and three millions are continually ill. If such figures could be gathered, clearly enough those actually disturbed by bodily ills run into many, many millions. And this was only for the United States.

Is it God's will to heal our bodies to-day? There's surely need enough. And He *can* do it. Will He? Does He want to? Is it in His heart and purpose to do it?

May I put the result of many years of study, and of observation in many nations, and of experience, into a single sentence? Then we can dig up and put together a few of the facts that are the underpinning of that sentence.

And the simple sentence is this: *it is God's first will for every man that he shall be pure in heart, strong and noble in purpose, gentle in human contact, happy in circumstances, at peace in his inner spirit, and strong and well in body.*

A Blessed Healing Trail.

Now, we are talking about God's attitude in this matter. And so we naturally turn to God's Book. It is striking to find out how the other book, the Book of Life, tallies up with, and illustrates, this written book, as of course it would. For the Book of God is a part of the Book of Life. It grew up out of human life. These are our two chief books of study here.

It is striking to look, at once, at the original Eden picture of life. For that was God's own, unhurt by any after touch. There man was in perfect health of body and spirit, living in happy unbroken contact with his God-chosen helpmate, in a garden. There was fulness of life, perfect health, and such a thing as weakness or disease or death quite unknown.

The story of Job stands as a sentinel-teacher at the opening of this old Book of God. It stands at the outpost to guard and point the way.

It is clearly the earliest of these books in its writing. It is devoted to the sorest question of human life, that is, human suffering, *and* God's solution. We usually miss that " and."

There are two parts to the story, Job's suffering, and the outcome. We have been fed up on the first part, the suffering. The second part, the outcome, has been strangely ignored. Yet it is the bigger part, by all odds.

There is suffering indeed, in family, in circumstances, and then in body of a very grievous sort. Then the healing touch comes. And all is changed. Even the ash-heap becomes fragrant now, for it was the gateway to a new life of the spirit, and so to bodily health and vigour, and all else that came.

Job's story is put at the very gateway of God's Book, with this stirring message: it is God's will to heal the inner heart and life, *and* the body.

Now note that this blessed trail of healing runs through the older pages of the Book unbroken. The teaching trail and the healing trail persist throughout side by side.

It is a three-fold healing, protection from actual disease just at hand, the continuance of health and vigour through the unseen touch of

God, and the positive healing where disease had actually gotten in.

From Eve's recognition that it was through that touch on her body that weakness was overcome, and she was able to go through what has become the severest bodily test of life,[1] on through Abimelech's experience,[2] and Sarah's,[3] Rebekah's[4] and Rachel's,[5] and Moses' leproused hand,[6] and Miriam's leproused body,[7] the story runs.

And the remarkable experience of the Hebrew people, in Egyptian slavery and as they were being freed, in closest touch with contagious epidemics, reveals the unseen touch of God plainly there, giving unusual bodily vigour under sore physical stress, and protecting from disease.

There's an outstanding bit at the beginning of the training of the new messenger nation. Israel was to become the world's teacher-nation. And as they enter their long session of schooling special emphasis is laid on God's eager willingness to heal.

It comes first in the flush of the tremendous Red Sea deliverance, when they were peculiarly sensitive to impressions. In the tense plea that they keep in full touch with their Deliverer comes this:

[1] Genesis 4:1 with 3:16.
[2] Genesis 20:17, 18.
[3] Genesis 21:1, 2, with 11:30, and 17:16, 17.
[4] Genesis 25:21.
[5] Genesis 29:31, 30:22-24.
[6] Exodus 4:6-7.
[7] Numbers 12:9-15.

"I will put none of the diseases upon thee which I have put upon the Egyptians; for I am the Lord that healeth thee."[1]

There was the triple healing, protection from, the touch of continuous health, the actual healing where disease had gotten in.

Then under the hush and awe of the lone Mountain, all aflame with the presence of their wondrous God, in the midst of a yearning plea to them to keep in touch with Him, this word rings out:

"I will take sickness away from the midst of thee. There shall none cast her young, nor be barren in thy land: the number of thy days I will fulfil."[2]

So the trail persists. Solomon remembers it in the great temple prayer.[3] There's Elijah and the widow's only son,[4] and Elisha with another mother's son,[5] and with Naaman,[6] and Hezekiah's never-to-be-forgotten story.[7]

There's Asa's failure to ask for needed healing, with the implied criticism,[8] and Nebuchadnezzar's recovery from insanity by direct touch,[9] and Jonah's grateful experience with that shady palm, and his remarkable preservation inside the huge fish.[10]

[1] Exodus 15:26.
[2] Exodus 23:25-26.
[3] 1 Kings 8:37-38.
[4] 1 Kings 17:17-24.
[5] 2 Kings 4:17-20, 32-37.
[6] 2 Kings 5:8-15.
[7] 2 Kings 20:1-11; Isaiah 38:1-21.
[8] 2 Chronicles 16:12.
[9] Daniel 4:24-37.   [10] Jonah 1:17-2:10, 4:6.

Christ's Will to Heal To-day   31

David's heart repeatedly rings out the same music in a sweetly rhythmic monotone.[1] One bit in particular stands out for the fulness and richness of its tone.[2] Let me paraphrase it to make the meaning in David's mind a bit closer home.

Listen:

"Who forgiveth all thine iniquities;
Who healeth all thy diseases;
Who keepeth thee from going down to the grave before thy full span of life is run out;
Who crowneth thee with loving kindness and tender mercies;
Who satisfieth thy matured years (when mental and spirit depression is apt to come) with the renewal of vigour until thou art as eager in spirit as an eagle soaring through the vast aerial heights."

Here are five things named. The first is spiritual. The fourth refers to the outer circumstances of one's life. The other three have distinctly to do with bodily health and vigour.

There's a choice bit from the pen of the wisest man before he became the stupidest of moral fools.[3] The revision gives this, " a tranquil heart is the life of the flesh."

Literally it reads, "the life of the body? a

[1] Psalms 6: 2, 30: 2, 3, 34: 20, 41: 2, 3 (a touch of the disciplinary side), 91: 3-7, 10-13.
[2] Psalm 103: 1-5.
[3] Proverbs 14: 30.

quiet heart." Our psychological friends would find much here for their side of things.

The processes of grace are fascinating. Full touch with God gives the quiet heart that passeth mere mental understanding, and that in turn acts directly on all the bodily functions.

And the trail runs eagerly ahead into the future glories never out of the Hebrew vision. The coming Messiah-King is to bring these physical blessings, along with all others.

Isaiah's exultant song of the coming day (in chapter thirty-five) may be taken as an index to the long list. The blind and the deaf, the lame and the dumb, will know all these disabilities completely gone.[1]

Rare Ezekiel's remarkable river, from trickling beginnings to flood, carried exuberant physical life and healing everywhere. And the leaves of the trees it fed would be a healing potion for all.[2]

The whole of these older pages makes one rhythmic answer to our question. They reveal plainly and graphically *God's attitude*. He not only can heal, but it is His eager wish to do so. His love outruns His power.

And always there's the eager reaching through bodily healing to the deeper, the richer, the spirit healing. The disciplinary side of suffering is plain. It's a wooing process. Through these silent pleadings and teachings of suffering God reaches in for the deeper.

[1] Isaiah 35:5, 6.
[2] Ezekiel 47:9, 12.

Teaching for Church Days.

But there's another bit of this old Book that concerns us people living now, most intimately. These older pages reveal the one unchanging God. He is ever the same.

But there's a book of illustrations of this same God which belongs peculiarly to us. It is distinctively *the Church book* of the Bible. I refer, of course, to the Book of Acts, with the Epistles woven in, and the Revelation knot on the end.

In the Gospels Christ reveals the heart of the Father. He gives the meaning vividly of these Old Testament pages. The Acts continues the story, for all the peoples, of all the world, who come into living touch of heart with Christ.

Acts is the sequel to the Gospels. The Gospels are sample pages of the coming Kingdom time, Acts sample pages of the Church time. Each covers a generation of time.

In the Gospels the King is pleading for acceptance. His ministry is an eloquent plea. In all He does, He is saying, "this is a bit of what the Kingdom is like." But the King is rejected, and goes voluntarily to the Cross to give His life out for men, and for their sins.

Then something new comes in. It is never spoken of in the Old Testament. It fills in the interregnum until the King shall bring in the Kingdom. The messenger-nation fails.

Now, a new group is formed to be God's new messenger to the race. It is called the Church, the "taken-out" group. It is formed of all be-

34   About the Healing Christ

lievers in Christ, both Jew and non-Jew, by the Holy Spirit's presence.

There's a natural contrast or comparison between the Gospels and the Acts. The Gospels are Kingdom pages; the Acts the Church book. Acts runs through a generation of time, roughly thirty-three years.

Then it breaks abruptly off, as though each generation of the Church should carry on the story, until Christ comes for the next step in His racial program.

In the Gospels healing has the foremost place in Christ's activity. But it does not come into prominence until Christ's rejection by the leaders is quite clear. There's over a year of waiting for national acceptance. Then Christ's official herald is imprisoned. That means Christ's own rejection.

Now, Christ turns to Galilee, unofficial Galilee, despised by the cultured Jerusalem leaders. He begins preaching and teaching and healing the crowds, and training the inner group of disciples.

When the national rejection of His Messiahship is quite clear He turns to the personal side of the Messiah's work. Healing now takes the prominent place. It is through healing that He first gets the great thronging crowds.

In the Acts healing has a distinct place, but on the whole not as prominent a place as in the Gospels. It becomes one feature only of the gracious ministry described, and of the power experienced. It *is* one feature. It is quite distinct in itself. Yet it becomes one feature with the others.

There are five summaries. These indicate that vast crowds experienced healing. All sorts of cases were included, great power clearly in action, and a deep abiding spiritual effect on the people.

There are eight individual instances of healing. One would be classed as acute. One was the supernatural protection from a deadly viper. Six are incorrigible incurables: twice lameness from birth, one of forty years standing; once long-standing palsy; twice the dead are brought back to life; and possibly Paul's recovery from stoning would be included with this last item.

There are two outstanding centres of healing activity, Jerusalem the Jew centre, and Ephesus the Galilean or non-Jewish centre. The Jerusalem activity is at the beginning, and the Ephesus activity distinctly toward the close, of the Acts period.

At Jerusalem great crowds are healed, great healing power is in evidence, and great spiritual blessing is connected with the healing.

At Ephesus the activity runs through two full years. The power in evidence is quite unusual, to a very marked degree. And the spiritual power in men's lives is quite pronounced.

Ephesus was the strategic center of Asia Minor. The message preached, and the power revealed there, went out to all parts of Asia Minor, and across the seas in every direction.

It is striking to mark that healing has greater

prominence in the record, in the space given it, at the beginning of Acts. Practically it tallies with the story of the Gospels. It continues a distinct part of the activity clear to the abrupt ending of the Acts.

But one is conscious that it becomes one feature with others. The absorbing thing here is the preaching of the crucified risen Christ. The healing becomes one manifestation with others of the power of the risen Christ.

Yet, there is no suggestion of the lessening of the power in healing, nor of minimizing its place. For it is toward the close of the Acts period that the unusual story comes of the young man who fell down dead out of the window at Troas, and is restored to life. And the outstanding Ephesus campaign is likewise toward the close. It is merely a shift of proportionate emphasis.

The Epistles fit into the pages of Acts, and are most intelligently read and understood as they are read in that way. They run side by side with Acts, with Revelation coming a bit later as the knot on the end of the whole.

Corinth becomes the strategic centre of European activity, as Ephesus is the strategic centre of the Asiatic. And as Ephesus had a special message of healing *activity,* Corinth sends out a special message of healing *teaching*.

Much space is given to the active ministry of the whole group of disciples in Corinth. It was clearly an active church centre, with the power of the Holy Spirit distinctly marked.

Christ's Will to Heal To-day 37

Distinct prominence is given to teaching about healing. Clearly healing was a blessed commonplace in the experience of these Corinthian Christians. And many among them had marked power in this regard in ministering to those in bodily suffering.

Healing is spoken of as one of the nine or more special gifts of the Holy Spirit. It was *one* of the gifts. There were other gifts. It was given to some, but not to all.

Here is the same sense of proportionate emphasis as in the Book of Acts. It was a blessed gift, one of several. Paul is putting special emphasis on *poise* in teaching, keeping things well balanced, in due proportion.

Toward the close of this Acts-Paul period there are distinct touches of some not healed. Paul's thorn comes in here. These will come in for treatment in the story of "God's School of Suffering,"[1] touching the disciplinary side of suffering.

The thing to mark just now is that they in no way change or affect the main teaching about healing. They simply give light to keep things in poise.

From of old, a common teaching has been that miracles ceased long ago, and are not to be expected. And this is quoted regarding healing.

This Book of Acts, with the interwoven Epistles, gives the clear answer. The interwoven Acts and Epistles make up the Church book, indicating what is meant to be the blessed

[1] See Chapter 7.

commonplace clear to the end of the Church period.

From the outer non-Jewish world, where these letters mostly take us, there is a quick turn back to things at the Jew centre.

The first Bishop of Jerusalem reveals the custom and the teaching that continued in the old mother Church. There was plainly no lessening of the teaching there, nor of the blessed experience.[1]

Then the circle of this wondrous old twin-book of God swings back to the starting point. There's a garden at both ends, Genesis and Revelation. God's ideal persists clear to the end, and becomes real, actual.

The tree of life has become a grove of trees. The garden has become a garden-city. All the fine simplicity of the country and the garden is coupled with all the fine true culture for which the city characteristically stands.

And here is the same winsome touch regarding our bodies. Sickness and pain, tears and death, mourning and crying, these are gone, clean worn out. The trees of life bear monthly harvests, and their leaves, like Ezekiel's, are for healing.[2]

The Answer of the Book.

All this is simply giving us a picture of God, a portrait in oil, in warm living colours. And that is the one point of the question we're talking about.

What sort of a God is He? What is He will-

[1] James 5: 13–15.   [2] Revelation 21: 4, 22: 1–2.

ing to do? It is not a question of power, but of His willingness, His purpose. Not *can* He? But *will* He?

The picture in the Old Testament is quite enough to answer the question. The warmer living colours of a Man actually living in touch, underscores the answer in bright red colouring.

The tenderness, the sympathetic heart, the eagerness of God, takes hold of one's heart with a grip as His Only-Begotten actually becomes one of us.

And so we come back to that sentence put in at the first. *It is God's first will that we should be pure in heart, gripped by a nobly strong purpose, poised in our understanding of things, humanly gentle in our personal contacts, at sweet peace within, content in circumstances, and hearty and healthy in our bodies.*

But note that word "first," God's *first* will. There will be a Quiet Talk devoted entirely to the meaning of that word "first." That's a doorway into God's schoolroom.[1]

Christ does heal to-day. It is His eager will to do so, and to do it now. One may reach out his hand, and have what he needs of this sort, now as he is reading, *so far as God's side is concerned.*

If there be any delay, it need not be longer than it takes for a man to come into simple full touch of heart and life.

In healing Christ is thinking of two things, always two. The first presses in most with us,

[1] See Chapter 7.

if we're needing it, maybe needing it sorely. The second is really the thing of greater meaning.

Christ wants to heal our bodies. He wants to heal our spirits, our lives, our real selves. He wants to do the first, but in such a way as to include the greater thing, the second.

The first is delayed sometimes, oftentimes, until we are willing for the second, too. But the length of the delay is fixed by us. Christ eagerly reaches out to do both for each of us now.

There is one exception to be noted in all this teaching. We are never promised immunity from bodily death. There are the three instances in the Gospels of the dead restored, and two, possibly a third, in the Acts.

Yet, the plain teaching throughout does not include this. A bit of the promise definitely made is, that through the touch of Christ on the body, the full span of natural life will be filled out.[1]

So far as death itself is concerned the resurrection of our bodies at some future day is plainly taught for those believers who do not live until Christ's return. The teaching does not go beyond these two items.

Now a bit from the other book, the book of illustrations, the Book of Life.

A friend of mine told me a bit of his experience of bodily healing. It's a double story. He is a business man, still living, well known in the

[1] Note Psalm 103:4 f. c. see paraphrase already given. Exodus 23:26. Deuteronomy 4:40, 32:47.

city where he lives, and active in Christian service of the more spiritual sort. He is now probably in his late fifties or early sixties.

In his thirties he had a stroke of paralysis, as a result apparently of overwork. It affected one side. His arm hung limp though not wholly disabled. He could walk some, dragging his limb.

The side of his face was affected. Through loss of self-control the spittle would ooze out of his mouth. He showed me his diary which he was still able to keep. But the writing on the pages at this time was a scarcely legible scrawl.

He went to a friend, a physician, who taught that Christ heals by direct touch as of old. The friend made a very simple brief prayer for his healing. And my friend limped out of the other's home as he had limped in, and started back to his own home.

As he was painfully dragging his foot along he felt a sense of warmth come into his body, running through his affected side, down the arm, and as though out at his finger-tips. And he knew the healing touch had come.

He entered his home with his latch-key, and his wife came running to meet him, and then stopped short as she looked, startled, and said, "Oh, Frank, you have been healed!"

My friend had unusually intimate relations with his pastor who lived near him. The pastor had suffered for years from heart trouble. He had applied repeatedly for life insurance with various companies. But had always been rejected because of his heart.

Now, my friend went to see his pastor, and told his story of what had just occurred to him. And there was a time of praise and prayer together.

The pastor was the more deeply impressed because of his own need. Much time was spent alone in his study on his knees with the open Bible. And he had evidence within that led him to believe the healing touch had come.

Again he applied for life insurance, was examined with the usual rigid care, and now was accepted, and the insurance written.

He began to speak of healing in his preaching. But it was not acceptable to his denominational leaders. And so it was not taught in any outstanding way, and gradually slipped out of his preaching.

He afterward became president of a leading Methodist university, and later was made bishop, and was prominent in the broader counsels and activity of his communion. I had the privilege of his personal acquaintance in the after years.

My friend, a quiet-spoken methodical business man, told me the story quietly, with a business man's care in details. He has led a very busy life since, and seems to be in perfect health.

It seems like an added page of the unfinished Book of Acts. Clearly there would be many more such pages added if our great Christ had His way with us.

III

DOES GOD SEND SICKNESS AND DISEASE?

It is God's first will that every man be clean in heart, in the grip of a noble purpose, clear in understanding of things, at peace within himself, gentle in spirit, happy in circumstances, and strong and vigorous in his body.

Essentials and Incidentals.

CHRIST was a man of power, and is. This is His distinctive characteristic. It was power under the driving control of love, and is.

The religion of Christ is a religion of power. This is its outstanding feature. It was through this that it won its way in the beginning, in the bitter competition with old entrenched religions. It was this that blazed its pioneer way into every nation and civilization where it has gone.

It is a power clearly above any power men were accustomed to. It is distinctly more and greater than men had known. It rose above power working commonly through familiar natural channels.

And so it is called supernatural power. It was plainly claimed to be the power of Christ Himself, and of God back of and through Christ, at work through natural channels.

And always it came into play to help men. The help was sorely needed. Men were powerless to do what was needed.

About the Healing Christ

This more-than-natural power of Christ, and of the religion of Christ, met men's sore need, and met it with a strange glad fulness. It was this distinctive trait that opened the doors and hearts and lives where the power was felt and seen.

Christianity is not a code of ethics, simply. It is that, plainly. It leaves all other codes trailing behind. Indeed there is pretty clear evidence that all these other codes sprang out of the mother roots of Christianity.

But, by comparison, this is merely a by-product, a blessed by-product. The distinctive thing is that Christianity is a religion of supernatural power.

It is not merely a system of culture. Very clearly it is that. The Holy Spirit's sway in a life brings the rarest culture of character and conduct. It leads to the truest culture of mind and personality and life. And this multiplied in many individual lives makes a rarely cultured community.

Its culture is the real thing, culture of heart and motive and behaviour and outreach to others. It clean out-cultures all other cultures, familiar to man. Its culture, at root, planted and fertilized all real culture wherever and whenever found. The evidence regarding this is abundant and clear.

But, in comparison with this other trait common to true Christianity, its culture is an incidental, a winsome wondrous incidental. The essential trait goes deeper in, and reaches farther out. Its power to transform personal life stands first and alone.

Christianity is not a teaching and a philosophy only. It surely is a teaching. It is a tremendous, a pervasive and satisfying philosophy.

All men, and all philosophers, and all nations, that know it gladly burn their incense at the altars of its teaching and its philosophy, the incense of words, and the greater incense of imitation.

There is the best of evidence for believing that the directly untraceable tendrils of all other philosophies and teachings run back to the Hebraic roots whence Christianity grew.

And this is still true, regardless of the strange unhallowed admixtures in these other systems. By common consent the teaching and philosophy of Christianity clear overtops all others.

Yet, be it keenly marked, again this is not the chief thing in Christianity. There is something greater back of this. It is so much greater as to have no second.

It's in a class by itself. Christianity is a thing of more-than-natural, more-than-human, power. It reveals God's own power in action through natural human channels.

There is even a stronger word to add here. Christianity is not a humanitarianism, a scheme for bettering world conditions, simply. It is that, clear beyond what can be told.

A simple quick run *back* in history to pre-Christian times, and a quick run *out* to non-Christian civilizations to-day, makes a startling contrast between nations that have come in any degree under Christian influence, near or remote, and the others.

Humanitarianism in all its blessed forms, and the unselfish bettering of outer conditions, stand out so big under Christian touch as to seem almost absent elsewhere.

Yet the distinct though faint traces elsewhere, even though untraceable directly, bear every mark of springing from the same old Eden-Hebrew-Christian rootage. Christ's humanitarianism is the root actually of all this sort of thing.

Yet, a moment's clear, sharp thinking makes quite plain that these blessed things that have meant so much, and do beyond all calculation, are still—yes, again the word comes—incidentals.

They are the sweet, refreshing fragrance of the rose. The rose itself, creating fragrance, and lavishingly breathing it out into the sweetened air, this is quite another thing. The rose is always immeasurably greater than the fragrance it gives unselfishly out to all comers.

Power the Distinctive Trait.

Christianity itself, in its one outstanding characteristic, is immeasurably more than the humanitarianism it initiates and keeps going. Its singular outstanding trait is its supernatural power, found nowhere else. It does what no other does or can do. It stands solitary and alone in this.

And, *and,* are you listening with your inner

ears? *And,* if and when, it loses this, in our understanding and our teaching of it, the essence is gone.

The fragrance is here; the rose is gone. What fragrance there is is what lingers from past contact with the real thing. How long will it linger with its source cut off?

If and when our Christianity becomes a code of ethics merely, a culture and only that, a teaching and philosophy and nothing more, a blessed humanitarianism and bettering of outer conditions of life, and that simply, the distinctive trait has gone.

The rose is severed from the fragrance. The life has gone out of the body, even with some colour in the cheek, and some muscular movements in the limbs.

The tendrils are severed from the life-giving roots. The Christian religion has been dragged down to the level of mere man-made religion, so far as the leaders can do that.

All these other things, so blessed in themselves, are mere by-products of Christianity, incidentals. One had almost said, trifling incidentals, by comparison, though so invaluable in themselves.

Christianity is distinctively, idiomatically, a thing of power, supernatural power, God's own direct touch through human natural channels. The lustful man is made pure. The slave of evil habit is set free.

The thief becomes honest. The trifler becomes earnest, in the hard grip of a noble purpose. The drunkard is sobered, and stays sober. The demon-tortured man knows sweet peace. The diseased is made perfectly whole.

Where there had been a man in the house, now there's a loving husband, and a thoughtful father, in a home. And the shop or store, the neighbourhood, the community, the nation, each knows a radical difference, a new personality, strong, gentle, pervasive, insistent.

The religion of the solitary God-Man who died, and then revealed unprecedented and unparalleled power, uncopiable by others, in emptying that new-hewn tomb of rock, it is a religion of supernatural power. It is a power unexplainable except by taking God into account.

It makes changes in man. It changes things at the core. Then all becomes changed. All history and all observation and all experience make clear enough that those changes can't be made by any other than Christ Himself. But Christ does. He only can. Christianity is distinctively a religion of supernatural power.

The one purpose of foreign missionary activity is to carry this message of the Christ, to our racial kinsmen across the sea who haven't heard.

It is distinctively the message of a Christ who died as none other did, nor could, nor can, and then lived again through supernatural power, and still lives, with that same supernatural power available to-day to purify the heart, transform the life, and meet every common need.

This was the one burning passion and purpose of the early missionary activity, and still is, where the Christ spirit sways. It burns so hotly and grips so strongly that all else seems the merest incidental.

There is an "else." There are incidentals. There are humanitarian activities immeasurably valuable and sorely needed. There are some things worked out by Western science that will alleviate living conditions over yonder. And that sort of thing is surely sorely needed. Yet there needs to be discrimination. And wise discrimination sometimes seems scarce.

It is no part of the Christian missionary scheme to transplant Western civilization into Oriental lands. The Orient has a culture of its own, that even some of us Occidentals think fully equal to the best true Western culture, at least, and in some things distinctly superior.

If our missionary activity become a mere transplanting of certain features of the Western hemisphere to Eastern and sub-equatorial lands, it at once loses its distinctive historical Christian characteristic. The essence has gone.

If the door opened with such sacrifice by the early heroic missionaries becomes an entrance for some common features of our Western civilization, if it become a means of spreading Western skepticism and doubt under Christian phraseology, it is surely the Devil using that door. Such use makes the door a distinct curse, so far.

The motive for such sacrifice as the true Christian missionary gladly makes, though it takes his life's blood slowly given out, that motive is quite gone.

The true Christian message lived and taught on foreign-mission soil, in the supernatural power of the Holy Spirit, will work out certain results.

Out of it will grow naturally the true Christian culture. *And* out of that will grow the *mental* regeneration that will affect daily life and conditions. And our racial brothers yonder will be distinctly better off with none other, except some products of Western science already alluded to.

Nowhere is the distinctively supernatural power of Christ revealed more than in this, that men's bodies are healed. It was so in Christ's day on earth. It was so in the early Church days. It is so to-day. Christ is still and ever the same.

Of course, there is opposition to such a Christ, and to such a religion. It was marked in Christ's day. It was bitter, incorrigible, malicious, and at last murderous.

A False Common Impression.

That opposition hasn't ceased. It has merely changed its outer form. It has grown more cultured on the outside, but the inside is the same.

One phase of this opposition is the teaching that God sends sickness and disease. The bald statement gives an ugly impression of God that stings and stays. It hurts and it lasts.

There comes a dread, an inner deep dread of a God of resistless power who actually does such a thing. This is so even among saintly Christians, far more than is suspected.

Its practical effect has been to act as a check to the working in men's lives of that supernatural power of Christ. The hand doesn't reach out to take what the Pierced Hand is eagerly reaching down to give.

There is a deep-seated impression that we cannot ask for healing. We must settle down and make the best of a bad thing. And meanwhile pray to be patient and resigned.

Psychologically this becomes an unconscious incalculable influence in actually tightening the hold of disease on one's body. Practically it makes a hindrance in the working of God's rare supernatural power in our bodies, and in our lives.

"Well, it was her time to go, and so God sent her pneumonia." The words were spoken quietly, in a matter-of-fact way, and in a tone of finality. They were the answer to my sympathetic question about an earnest Christian woman in the prime of life who had died quite unexpectedly.

I wondered if my startled ears heard aright. But my wife verified their accuracy. The woman who spoke the words was an earnest Christian, of much more than average culture. Several of her family circle were college-bred, and the home had an unusual supply of high-class modern books of various sorts.

In later conversation a neighbour of hers, who did not share her belief in this regard, remarked that such was quite a common thought in all the countryside thereabouts. And in varying degree one finds such impression deep-seated everywhere.

And, there are statements in the Scriptures that can be distorted, and disconnected, to give such an impression. That is, I mean, with no intention of distorting, the Scriptures are read in a haphazard, disjointed way, and are quoted without regard to connection. And so such impressions gotten by hearsay are deepened.

The Teaching of the Book.

Let us take a brief look at the Book on this point. There's a long list of passages that, taken by themselves, at first-flush, do give that impression. But as one reads them in connection with the whole teaching he feels ashamed so to have misunderstood God's word, and really maligned, though unintentionally, God's character.

When Abraham and Sarah went into Egypt it says plainly, "Jehovah plagued Pharaoh and his household with great plagues because of Sarah, Abraham's wife."[1] The word "plagues" here plainly means certain contagious diseases common in Egypt.

The whole story tells plainly why. God's plan for the new nation hinged on Abraham, and even more on his wife, and on the family

[1] Genesis 12: 10–20.

stock being kept pure. It was really an emergency in the human plan being worked out. And the broader story tells the process which reverses the whole impression. Still the impression is there, to the unthinking.

There's God's dealings with Pharaoh in delivering Israel from Egyptian slavery. One cannot go here into this whole story of judgment on the Egyptians for their conduct toward God, and toward these Hebrews.

That's another story, much misquoted, and often not thoughtfully read, and full of fascinating interest. It reveals in a notable way *the natural process* God follows in visiting judgment on wrong-doing.

But it plainly says that it was through "the hand of the Lord" in direct action that the Egyptian cattle were fatally diseased, and the Hebrews' cattle immune; the ulcerous boils upon the Egyptians themselves, and so on, through all the plagues that follow.[1]

One notes, of course, that this is all a distinctly exceptional action, of judgment, in a crisis. It is not the normal run of things. Still the impression spoken of may remain if one doesn't think the thing out as plainly taught. And so there is a string of similar passages.[2]

There is one exception to be noted, quite distinct from all these others. That's the story of

[1] Exodus 9: 1-7, 8-12.
[2] Exodus 15: 25-26, 32: 35, Leviticus 10: 1-2, Numbers 11: 1, 33, 12: 9-15, 14: 12, 36, 37, Deuteronomy 28: 21, 22, 27, 35, 60, 61, and others.

Jacob's hip being put out of joint.[1] One notes at once that it was not a disease, but a touch that affected the normal action of his body, his walking.

It slowed him up, and became a constant reminder that he *had been* walking the wrong way. And now, though his walking is slower, it is in God's way, the only right way, and is so wholly because of that strange midnight touch. There is no wasted motion now.

It stands out as an exception, at the extreme point of waiting by God, after all other means had failed. Jacob was an unusually stubborn man. It was for service' sake, and was in an emergency in God's world plan, of which this man was the human center. It will be spoken of again in the Talk on "God's School of Suffering."

The Protected Zone.

Now, there are two things to note sharply here in order to keep the poise, to get things straight and clear. And they are two common things, well understood and emphasized *in the pages of this book.*

The first, and less thing is this, that any break with God takes one away from the protection of His presence, and so automatically exposes him to whatever conditions surround him.

The natural thing is *keeping in touch* with God. His mere presence, in unbroken touch, is a continual protection from ills that surround

[1] Genesis 32: 24–32.

Does God Send Sickness? 55

us. His touch upon us, it is this that keeps our bodies strong, and functioning naturally and vigorously.

This teaching is like an ever-present undertone through the older pages of the Book. It was true from Eden on before the main story of the Book was lived out and written down. It is true to-day. This is the continual background of all the Old Testament teaching about bodily conditions.

One simple illustration may help. But it is merely one bit from a flood of passages. It is given because it is a picture, pictured teaching. It is an open window into the whole house of the Book.

It is the graphically told story of the unnamed prophet in the First Book of Kings.[1] He had been sent to King Jeroboam, in a very critical time, with a message, and with detailed instructions as to his own conduct. Clearly his own conduct in the particulars named was to be an acted-out bit of the message.

Another prophet, clearly merely a professional prophet, jealously deceived the man with God's message, who accordingly disobeyed God's explicit instructions. Then the unnamed prophet returning home, by the way he was distinctly bidden by God not to take, is slain by a lion.

The whole story is dramatically told in much detail of an intensely interesting sort. And is evidently told fully for the teaching it contains. For the whole nation knew the story by the

[1] 1 Kings 13.

universal grape-vine means of communication, and discussed it from door to door.

And the bit of teaching that belongs in just now is simply this: this unnamed prophet, in disobeying God's implicit directions, *had gone out of the protected zone.*

In touch with God he was in the protected zone. No evil could befall him in the simple path of obedience. He was protected. When he went out of that path he was exposed to the dangers always there.

The true natural human life is meant to be lived in simple touch of heart and life with God. Anything else is abnormal, unnatural. When in touch one is constantly protected and preserved and strengthened, in body and circumstance and life.

Break with God, either partial or full, exposes one to whatever there is of evil, and to the Evil One. And, it is an unhappy commonplace that so many Christians, confessedly, do not live in that full simple intelligent touch with Christ in all their affairs.

This is one bit of teaching. It is the background of all teaching in the Old Testament especially. Unhappily it is missed so much in the haphazard, unconnected, choppy reading of the old Book, so common in pew and pulpit, home and study.

It is a striking thing that the Bible, taken as a whole, is always self-explanatory Any question raised at any place in it as to the meaning is always answered somewhere else in the Book.

Does God Send Sickness?   57

And every thoughtful, serious question has an answer here somewhere. If only we would *read* it, and read it *intelligently as a whole,* one connected book, it would flood us with its light at every turn.

But the second thing stands out in plain open day before all eyes. It is the bigger thing of the two. It is the Book of Job. The story of Job deals directly with this question of sickness and disease, the source, and more the purpose.

It stands at the front door of the Bible. It was first of all in its writing. It is put there in plain sight that we might understand at once this sorest of all questions, suffering, and why allowed.

It tells plainly that the troubles that came to Job, including his ulcerous boils at the last, came directly from Satan.[1] Though Job himself didn't so understand, and ascribed them to God.[2]

They came distinctly by God's permission. There were sharply defined limits to Satan's activity, beyond which he could not, dare not, go.[3] There was a purpose of God in the permission He gave. It was distinctly a purpose of love. Then the healing came.[4] And the gracious flood of blessing that followed made the days of his earlier prosperity seem tame.

That in a word, just now, is the Job story.

[1] Job 1:12-19, 2:6-7.
[2] Job 1:20-21, 2:10.
[3] Job 1:12, middle clause, 2:6.
[4] See Job 33:15-25, see paraphrase in Chapter 7, "God's School of Suffering." Job 42:10-17.

It comes in for more in the Talk on "God's School of Suffering."

But the teaching could not be clearer. It answers our present question. It answers it fully and plainly. And the teaching stands at the front door of God's Book, that all who will simply read thoughtfully may understand. Of course, it must be confessed that reading the Book of God is just a bit scarce, and reading it thoughtfully just a bit scarcer.

The Source of Disease.

Put in plain words here is the answer of the Book of God. God does not send disease and sickness. There are five things to be said about their source.

They come through some open door of disobedience to the laws of the body, either a conscious or an unconscious disobedience

Or, they may come directly from Satan, but always *through* some open door on the human side. *Or,* they may come through God's restraint being withdrawn.

Or, they may come through the general break of sin affecting the whole fabric of life. *Or,* there may be a blend of two or more of these.

In each case there must be an open door of some sort on the human side. But, then, the open doors are certainly on every hand in great abundance.

So far as the disciplinary side of bodily suffering is concerned, God has no need to send disease. There are plenty of doors of disobedience standing invitingly open to disease. There is no disobedience so common as disobedience of the common laws of health.

This is so among the most earnest Christians, the saintliest folk. There will be more said about this in the Talk on "The Human Side of Health and Healing."

We seem not to think into the common fact that breaking a law of one's body, though not against a moral law, yet takes on a distinctly moral quality. The laws of health are God's laws for the body, as really as moral laws are His for the life.

God's healing, it will be remembered, is threefold. There is a protective restraint of which one may be quite unaware. One's person is protected. There's a distinct restraint on the disease just at hand threatening.

There is the life-giving, health-giving touch upon one's body, giving vigour and full functioning. And of this touch one is usually quite unaware. The very absence of bodily ills and weakness should be cause for praise. It reveals Christ's direct touch, where the body is committed to His care.

And, then, when sickness or disease actually comes, perhaps through some door left inadvertently open, or otherwise, there may be the positive supernatural healing touch.

When one is led to meet some emergency that taxes or exposes the health unduly special strength will be given. But one should be very clear of his leading here. Once that is quite clear one pushes confidently on, depending on our unfailing Christ for bodily strength, as for all else.

But one should guard carefully his bodily doors, as all others. There is a spirit warfare on. And one needs to be constantly on guard. In a wholesome, sane, thoughtful way one should guard all the doorways of his life, of every sort. This is especially true of those wholly in Christian service.

John Ruskin tells a simple incident of his childhood days, that illustrates in part what we are talking about. He was present one afternoon when tea was being served.

The copper hot-water kettle was bright, and caught the child's eye. He wanted to touch it, and reached out his hand. The nurse in attendance on the child told him not to. The boy persisted, and the nurse also persisted.

By and by the mother said quietly, "Nurse, let him touch it." He did, for a very brief moment. His curiosity was quickly satisfied. His attention was turned from the kettle to the finger.

The child's ignorant persistence in having his own way, regardless of the expressed wish of those in authority, was deliberately yielded to for a purpose. The restraint was withdrawn. The act of touching the kettle contained its own punishment in the pain that came. The child had learned something. His desire to touch shining copper kettles was satisfied ever after.

But some of us haven't as much sense in

other similar things. We still want to touch the shiny kettle. God's commands and laws are never arbitrary. He doesn't simply want to be obeyed because He has the right to be. Though when you come to know Him, you recognize that this would be quite sufficient in itself.

But there's always a reason for our well-being involved. God would keep us from touching the hot kettle, because it will burn. This principle underlies every law and commandment of God to us.

An English friend told us of an experience she had. She was engaged in missionary work in Algiers, on the Mediterranean, at the time. An emergency led to her nursing a typhus patient for a brief time under quarantine regulations.

Then the patient was taken to the hospital. Our friend bathed, changed her garments, taking every precaution known to her, and retired for much needed sleep. She had a dream, unusually vivid and distinct in detail.

In her dream she was out riding, and saw a conflict going on between one of her missionary associates and three persons. She seemed to know instinctively that one of these three was the Devil himself.

She hastened forward to help her associate, but a dart was sent by one of the group of three. And her associate fell as she came between them. Almost mechanically she prayed, repeating the words "the power of the blood of Jesus."

At once the three fell back. Then they came

again to the attack. Again she prayed, repeating that same phrase, but apparently without realizing its full significance and power. And again the three fell back.

The third time they pressed up in attack. Then it came to her swiftly, with an intense sense of reality, just what power there was in that prayer, pleading "the power of the blood of Jesus."

Pleading it now boldly, strongly, insistently, the three crouched down and back as though struck. Then slowly, reluctantly, but surely, they disappeared. And her associate was free of their power.

That was the unusual dream. It stood out with singular distinctness. She awakened, and found herself in a high fever. Then the significance of the dream seemed borne in upon her.

She engaged in prayer, in tense insistent prayer, pleading the power of the blood of Jesus. Then sleep came quiet and deep. When she awakened the fever was quite gone. Her pulse and temperature were normal. She was quite cool and well. And with grateful heart she went about her day's task.

Let us keep in touch of heart and life with Christ, guard jealously all the doors, set ourselves to keep in that protected zone of obedience, *and,* when the need comes go at once to Christ.

Christ is waiting now, at your side, with the touch of supernatural power, to meet every need of body and life.

IV.

HOW DOES CHRIST HEAL? THE CONDITIONS: THE METHOD: THE USE OF MEANS

It is Christ's first will for His followers, that they be pure in heart, strongly, steadily, passionate in purpose, poised in understanding and judgment, characteristically gentle in personal touches, willing to be controlled in everything by the emergency of sin in the world, and healthful and vigorous in body, to His glory.

Natural and Supernatural.

GOD is chary of the supernatural. He is lavish in nature. Nature is God in action. He loves nature's roads. He made them. He prefers them.

He will not hesitate for a moment to do the supernatural when the need calls for it. He will do a fresh act of creation, pure direct creation, before a single line of His Word is allowed to fail.

He will reach through and above the natural channels with the added touch before He will let one trusting child of His, in intelligent touch of heart and will, know disappointment. The flood of power, more than the usual thing, waits any emergency that plainly calls for it.

But, God loves nature's regular paths. They

are His own. Nature is God's way of working things out.

Christ avoids the sensational, the cheap, vulgar, catchy-in-the-bad-sense sensational. On more than one occasion He was at pains to avoid the crowd gaping for some touch of this morbid sort of sensationalism.

Though nothing is so sensational, in the good sense, as God's power in action in an unusual way in some sore emergency. Christ's miraculous healing created a tremendous sensation. And He made use of that sensation to teach of the Father's eager love, and gentle patience, and lavish power.

The supernatural has a touch of the spectacular to us, because we are not used to it. It is unusual. It catches attention at once. The natural hardly gets any attention, we are so used to it.

Nature is simple and quiet. The things that mean most to us, and to our daily lives, come noiselessly, softly. They work modestly. No one ever heard the sun or the moon, busily at work keeping the whole order of nature in blessed rhythm for our sakes.

The dew does its gracious work shyly. It's the small, warm, gentle rain that the soil welcomes most, and responds to most quickly. The air does its unfailing ministry so modestly we scarcely ever think of its presence, till some foul intruder spoils its sweet odour and neutralizes its life-giving power.

Truth is a Quaker. It wears a plain garb and

How Does Christ Heal? 65

talks in quiet gentle speech. It never calls attention to itself. It goes by almost unnoticed in the bustle of the street. But it breathes out a healthful atmosphere, and leaves a fragrant trail.

Error wears flashy clothes. It talks in loud, boisterous tones. It blusters, and swaggers the full width of the sidewalk. And the crowd stops and stares, and wists not that the air had been befouled. Error steals some truth for wings, else it would fall dead flat at once.

The Devil borrows truth's clothes, without asking permission. He talks in a loud, positive, there's-no-doubt-about-this voice. So men's eyes and ears may be caught and befouled.

The sheep-like quality persists in the race. Watch the flock of sheep. They'll follow the bell-wether unhesitatingly, even over the side of the bridge into the rushing river. Cheap, noisy leadership quickly gets the crowd.

Nature is simple. That's God's touch. Satan tangles things up. Truth is so simple as to seem too easy, sometimes. One instinctively says "of course." Sin makes life's problems complex. Truth is plain spoken and unpretentious. One becomes wary and weary of a cloud of words, many words, long, big-sounding words.

Christ is chary of the supernatural. He is lavish in nature. He gives so lavishly all the time that there would be no need of the other, the extra, the supernatural, if it were not for the terrible emergency of life.

Sin is forever setting life all askew, and making emergencies. A single touch of the supernatural quickly catches the eye. A flood of the natural, keeping the whole swing of life a-going, rarely gets a thought.

Yet, though already so lavish in His habitual giving, and so thoughtful about giving outside of this, Christ is on the eager run to give the more-than-common touch of power, the supernatural, when need be, to meet the ever present emergency so common in life.

Sin's ravages are epidemic. There's a wilful ignoring of the simple natural laws of the body. There's an ignorant disregard of nature's beneficent laws of action. There's a constant need of the supernatural touch. And Christ thoughtfully gives that touch in the way that will help us best and most.

Our well-being, body and spirit, is precious to Him. The integrity of His pledged Word He holds sacred. He is on the heels of evil, like a flash, before any trusting child of His shall be disappointed, or a scratch of His Word allowed to slip.

Helping So As Not to Hurt.

We've been talking about Christ's power in healing; what He *can* do. We've spoken of His love in healing; what He *will* do, and do with an eager gladness.

Now, we want to talk a bit together about Christ's wisdom in healing, the *way* in which He does heal. There's a rare wisdom in Christ's method in healing men's bodies.

How Does Christ Heal?

There is nowhere that wisdom is so much needed, rarest wisdom, as in giving. Those engaged in giving help to others habitually, in a larger or smaller way, know well what a fine art is needed here if men are not to be hurt when they are needing help.

To give so as to help, and help in the best way, and help only, not hurt, is a fine art indeed. Nothing is more ticklishly difficult. Thoughtless giving is cheap and common, lazy and hurtful. Love is always thoughtful, though it cost more. But love ignores the cost even when it must be counted.

In His healing, Christ is thinking always of two things, the immediate need and the deeper need, the body, and the man himself living in the body.

Often helping the deeper need meets the bodily need too, and meets it in the best way. The glad, intelligent surrender to Christ as a Master brings certain changes in one's habits. And this in turn radically affects the body and the health, oftentimes.

Often Christ's touch upon the life prepares the way for the touch upon the body. It does yet more. It leads to the intelligent thinking into things. And this in turn leads to such obedience to the laws of the body as to prevent a recurrence of the bodily trouble.

Sometimes that obedience is very simple. Sometimes it is radical. It may mean breaking old habits in such common things as eating and sleeping and the methodical daily round. And health and healing are very dependent on these common things.

Christ is love. And nowhere is love more put to it to be really helpful than in giving. The tangle of sin has come in to blur men's eyes, and teeter their judgment this way or that, and especially to make the will twisted and abnormally set in its way.

There are two things to note keenly here, as to how Christ heals. There are two "hows," the how of *conditions* and the how of *method*.

The conditions underlie all else. This has to do with one's touch with Christ. The method has to do with the healing itself, the way it's done.

The physician and the sick man must get into touch. Christ and the man needing Christ's healing power must get together.

Some have supposed that saintliness is the requirement for the healing touch. They have supposed that the saintly may come and expect the healing touch; but hardly others.

Well, of course, the closer the touch the better. And saintliness practically means simply a close touch, the habitual close touch.

But it isn't the saintliness that heals, nor because there is enough of it. There must be touch, of course. But it is Christ, Christ's blood, that heals.

It is never because of any merit in us such as saintliness suggests. It is *through* the contact, however saintly it may be or not, that Christ's healing power comes in.

The "How" of Conditions.

Now, the word *about the conditions* necessary for healing. Of course, there are always conditions. That's a bit of the common sense of life. Whether it's having a check honoured at the teller's window, or having the right to run an automobile,

Or, motoring through thick traffic in the city, or cooking a good meal, or playing golf, or keeping in good bodily shape, or polite social intercourse, or what not in the common run of life, there are always conditions.

And here the conditions are so simple as to be almost laughable. And yet they are so inflexibly rigid as to be absolutely indispensable, like almost all conditions of life.

Listen: come to Christ the Saviour, who died for our sins, as none other did, nor could, nor can. Ask for, and accept, forgiveness of your sins, and the cleansing from sin through His blood. Thank Him for dying for you and taking your sin away.

Then, when the need comes, go at once to Him. Whatever the need may be, cleansing from some sin you've let in, power to break that evil habit, guidance in some difficult situation, or bodily healing of whatever sort, to whatever extent, go to Him. Go first to Him. Go to Him at once.

He will forgive all our iniquities. He will heal all our diseases. He will prolong our days till the full span of life is run out. He will put His direct helpful touch on the outer circumstances, for our sake. He will renew the vigour of body and mind and spirit clear up to the measure it should be. This is His will for you and me.[1]

Now, it would be quite enough to stop right there. That tells the whole story of the conditions to be met.

But, because things are quite a bit foggy, it will be good to talk a bit about just what this means in actual habit, in the common run of things, in daily life.

We haven't been taught about healing. Indeed we haven't been taught much at all about the Christian life. There are always fine exceptions.

We need to be taught. Then there will be an intelligent understanding. There will come to be a matured mellowed mental judgment. There will be a seasoned wisdom to know how to act in emergencies. There will be a habit of action formed.

We will know how to meet opposition. We'll understand about "the fiery darts." For our enemy is cunning and practised. He's an old hand in the fine art of befooling, and filling the air with foggy questions and doubts.

An old seasoned soldier holds steady under fire when the new recruit takes to his heels. The experienced banker or broker keeps his head when panic threatens where the less-seasoned takes fright and maybe loses out.

So there's a bit more to say. It's detail. It's

[1] Psalm 103: 1–5.

included in what has been said. It will really grow up out of that *if* one follows fully and truly and simply. It can be put into four words, an *act*, a *purpose*, a *habit*, an *attitude*.

The *act* is the surrender to Christ as a master, not a Saviour simply but a master. In a thoughtful intelligent seasoned way Christ is to be allowed to sway all the habits, as the flame sways the dry kindling in the grate with a good draft.

The personal habits, the home relationships and contacts, the daily work, or business or profession, the income and out-go, the recreations and social contacts,—all these, in a wholesome sane habitual way, are to be as you believe He would prefer.

For He always has a preference, very decided. And when in doubt hold the thing in question open till the doubt quite clears.

The surrender is an act, a glad act. Then it becomes a practice, a constant unwavering practice. And then it becomes a habit, a fixed unconscious habit of action.

It simply means fullest touch of habit and motive and life with Him who died for us, out of the love of His heart, when He didn't have to. This is the meaning of being *in touch with Christ*.

The *purpose* is this: in everything to please Him. The purpose really becomes a passion, a tender, strong, tense passion, a passion of love, a passion for *Him*.

It does not simply ask "is this wrong?" and

leave it out. "Is this right?" and put it in. But this: "What would He prefer? What would please Him?"

There are many things that aren't wrong. You can prove that so far as logic goes. Though, of course, logic can be used to prove anything. And of course again, logic itself proves nothing.

A thing may be proven not wrong. But if that quiet inner Voice tells you it is not best, not what He would prefer, then that is quite conclusive here for the man really *in touch*.

Christ's preference, Christ Himself, the Man who loved so, and loves, and cares what we do, this quite settles things for the man *in touch*.

The *habit* is this: a bit of daily time off alone with the Book every day. The day may be crowded, but the man *in touch* finds that bit of time planned for, and growing longer of itself rather than shorter. What one really wants is always included, however crowded the day and the way.

It'll be time when the mind is fresh, or the nearest it comes to being fresh, whatever time that may be. It will be unhurried time, the spirit unhurried, even though the watch lies open before you.

It will be time with the Book itself. And if one has a paragraphed Bible (such as the revisions), with good clear type, a copy pleasant to handle, and if he isn't afraid to make notes on the margin so things will stand out, so much the better.

In that bit of time each day, multiplied by

as many days as the calendar provides, the vision clears, the understanding is taught, the purpose stiffens, the judgment seasons and acquires poise (that rarest thing!), the spirit gentles, the heart becomes purer and hotter (the normal heart condition), the brain cooler, the feet steadier, the up-reaching hand bolder, and the out-reaching hand warmer. This is what *keeping in touch* means.

The continual *attitude* of mind and spirit comes instinctively under the sway of all this. One goes the simple daily round with an unspoken prayer and an inner song.

There's the doing of the endless commonplace things with a new spirit. They're done for Him, as He did them in that Nazareth home and carpenter shop. The commonest things are done well because done under His eye.

There may be monotony in act, but never in spirit. What would be drudgery becomes rhythm, because of the inner spirit. The ever-present One within, the song in your heart even when clouds gather, these sweeten the humdrum task.

And when the unexpected comes, when the emergency suddenly looms, this quiet, steady attitude of spirit finds you ready. You are prepared. You hear the clear, quiet inner voice. You know instinctively what to do. And you hold still and steady till you do know. This is what *keeping in touch* means.

The whole thing is just that, being *in touch* with Christ, and *keeping* in touch. This is the simple underlying condition for healing. This being in touch is the natural human thing. Anything else is not human. It's an intrusion. Things are out of plumb.

This simple natural touch with Christ means health, a normal bodily functioning all the time. It means protection from that which threatens your health. It means the direct healing touch, if and when, disease actually gets in.

This is the first "how" of Christ's healing, the how of conditions, *getting and keeping in touch*. Sin broke and breaks the touch with Christ. We were started in touch back in Eden. We are born into this world in touch, at least, *creatively*. And that's no small thing.

The whole fabric of modern life, as it actually is, tends to the breaking of that touch. The wilful doing what we want to when we instinctively know we should do something else, this starts or strengthens the break.

Loss of touch means loss of strength, yes, bodily strength. And disease and sickness and weakness in general, in some way, come through that break.

Coming to Christ, coming all the way, and staying, this mends up the break. He mends it up. Then the way is open for all one needs of whatever sort.

And, when, some day He comes back again, there will be the fulness of touch in His immediate presence. Then the last lingering vestige of sin's break in our bodies will be gone.

The body laid away in the dust, in a believing hope, will know the fulness of life again, as will ours who are still living in that day.

The "How" of Method.

Then, there's the second "how" of healing, the *how of method*. What about the use of means? No question is more often asked in this connection. And there is the utmost confusion about the right answer.

When Christ was here there was no science of healing. There always has been a natural healing practised by men. The Jews have been noted for their skill in the use of herbs and other simples, and in nursing. Luke was in all probability such a physician.

To-day there is far more knowledge of the human body, and of the effects upon it of certain substances found in the vegetable world. There has grown up through years a fund of experience and of wisdom and skill in this regard. Properly used it is invaluable in discerning just what the ailment is, and what is wisest to do.

In spite of malpractice, wrong and faulty diagnosis, guesswork and experimentation, the unwise use of drugs, the commercialism, and the rapid putting of people through a wholesaling process in medical practice, and a not-good professionalism, in spite of these there is a human science of healing.

It is most striking that outstanding men in that science to-day put greatest emphasis on the non-use of drugs, on the sort and preparation and quantity of food, on the general habit of life, and on the mental attitude.

Above all else skill in accurate diagnosis, the actual discernment of just what the trouble is, is distinctly rare. It is rare in its common scarcity. And it is rarer yet in its value, its influence on needed action for relief.

There has grown up in recent years a new group of physicians, known by various names, who stress natural methods, the disuse of drugs, correcting wrong adjustments in the body by skilful manipulation, proper use of proper food, and like measures.

Without doubt, the Christian physician, studious and conscientious, dispassionately abreast of the latest real learning in his science, in real touch habitually with Christ, and under the sway of the Holy Spirit, free from the pride of mere professionalism,

Concerned only and above all in having his patient get well, with a simple faith in the present power of a living Christ, such a physician would be aided by the Holy Spirit in discovering the real ailment, and used in ministering to relief and healing.

But you say quickly, "Where is such a physician?" and I say, quite confidently, there have been such physicians, and there are. Though one regrets their scarcity, and prays most fervently that their number might be increased. For, be it keenly marked, this would be strictly in line with God's way of doing things. Their very absence or scarcity simply makes greater the need of going direct to the great Physician.

Here is a quotation from the lips of a physician, than whom it is said none stands higher in the profession in these two English-speaking nations. The quotation is a recent one, and is taken from a standard religious journal.

This famous physician said, "I believe that prayer does cure disease. Healing comes to some individuals directly through prayer, I am sure. I use it in my practise and rely on it today more often than on medicine. I believe that prayer is the contributing factor in the victory over disease.

"If I had no material means at hand I should use prayer alone, with confidence that it would work the cure, if recovery were in conformity with God's will. And when prayer has thus been made a factor in recovery I believe it is through direct action on the part of God."

The Seven Ways Healing May Come.

It will help much to remember here that there are seven different ways in which healing may come to the diseased body, four natural, two supernatural, one a blend.

There is a *natural healing without human co-operation.* The Creator has graciously put a healing power in the human body. If you cut your finger instantly nature goes to work. The blood begins to coagulate and staunch the flow. That power within begins to make new tissue, to bring the two edges of the wound together, and to heal it up completely.

This has been true, of course, since Eden days, through the centuries, and everywhere, in savage jungles and krall, and in cultured city centre.

There is this same *natural healing assisted by human coöperation*. A right mental attitude exerts enormous influence.

The term " subjective mind " is used for certain mental faculties and processes. The term " objective mind " is used for other mental faculties and processes or functions. Maybe some day the thing can be put into simpler words for us common folk to grasp more clearly. Mental science has not yet been fully charted.

Without doubt, the subjective mind, or the subjective functions of the mind, do control the sensations and functions of the body. The imagination plays an incalculable part here.

Again, without question, the objective mind or processes control the subjective mind as absolutely as the subjective mind controls the body. The body is the slave of the subjective mind in its instant, full, I had almost said, abject obedience to it. The subjective mind is the slave of the objective mind as absolutely.

Our knowledge, and reasoning, and deciding, and the insistent set-of-mind affect the imagination enormously. And this in turn actually controls in large measure bodily conditions.

Incidentally, just now, here is the *process of faith,* a simple faith in Christ, inbreathed by

His Holy Spirit, through His Word or more directly, as all faith is.

The objective mind lays hold of Christ's promise, and accepts unquestioningly the result as already quite assured. The subjective mind in obedience to that at once goes to work to produce the needed changes in the body.

Then, quite in addition to this, as the need may be, there is a supernatural touch of Christ's own direct power coming in, and working directly upon the body, and also working through this purely natural process.

The thing to mark just now is that the whole mental attitude, both conscious and unconscious, affects enormously the free working of that natural healing correcting power within every man's body. The processes of grace are as fascinating as a romance.

Then there is this *natural healing power assisted by expert knowledge and practised skill.* Here is where the true physician comes in. And the most a physician ever can do is to assist this natural healing power.

The wise physician recognizes this, and freely acknowledges it. He is merely nature's assistant. His best work is in finding out, what that natural power already knows, just what the trouble really is.

Then he can be of real assistance, and only then. Otherwise he is only a poor bungler hindering. And if he be sufficiently wise, and humble enough, and maybe sometimes unprofessional enough, merely to be an assistant, so far all is well.

And when healing comes what the assistant has done is distinctly the smaller part. That natural healing power has done the big thing, under a wondrous unseen personal Physician directly directing and aiding.

My eye was quickly caught with the legend cut deep into the gray stone over a large hospital building near one of our largest Eastern cities. It said "Man tends; God mends."

The truth got out that time. The big thing is done by God, that is, as is commonly said, by nature. Man's highest place is as an attendant. And surely it would be scientific and wise and good common sense for the attendant physician to be in closest sympathetic touch with his Chief-of-staff.

What a tragic thing for the poor patient when he isn't. This is the third way in which healing may come, the natural healing power within the body assisted by human skill.

Then there is a fourth way. The *natural healing, in spite of, and overcoming unwise bungling and lack of skill.* The human touch in this case puts a greater burden on the natural healing.

And oftentimes the burden proves too much. The human touch is an interference. Nature is outdone. And the poor patient limps slowly along, or his life slips its tether.

There are two supernatural ways in which healing comes. There is the direct supernatural touch of Christ, distinctly in addition to anything that nature or human skill or both can do. And this is the one thing which this series of Talks is mainly concerned with.

And there is a second supernatural healing, the Devil's. A strange thing this! That comes in for separate treatment in a later Talk.

And then, of course, there may be a blend of two or more of these. Four natural, two supernatural, and a blend of these two.

The Use of Means.

But, now, we come direct to the question: what about the use of means? And the answer is simple. And it is an answer that answers. There need be no evasion here, smothered up in foggy rhetoric.

The answer is this: *ask Christ*. Get in touch, if not already so. And then when the need comes ask Him. He will tell you. And if you are in touch, and you will listen quietly, you'll hear His answer, clear and simple and positive.

The dominant law of the Christian life, do you know what it is? This: obedience to the Holy Spirit's leading. This takes the first place, always. When there is any conflict this law displaces all others.

Perhaps you ask, but how shall one know just what His leading is? And that question has already been answered in that bit on keeping in touch. Four things were named for keeping in touch with Christ, act, purpose, habit, attitude.

That's the answer here. In that habitual

touch we will know clearly just what the Holy Spirit would have us do. And as we do what He tells us things will clear up for us yet more.

Christ heals through means and the skilled human expert, sometimes. He heals without these, sometimes. He heals when the physician frankly confesses his inability to cure. And sometimes He heals by overcoming and counteracting the physician and the means used.

Ask Him. He's there by your side, inside. He's intensely interested. He's eager to tell you what to do. In this He is a true physician, for He *advises*.

And, if it may be through means, remember it is His touch through the needed means that is effective. And His own personal direct touch is more, much more, than the means or the expert human counsel that He may know your body stands in need of.

The wise physician is an expert in the body, its functions and its needs. Your body may be needing something it isn't getting, may be needing it very badly.

Modern cookery, with some exceptions, is washing out of the food chemical salts and other nourishment that our bodies need for health and strength.

Modern commercialism, for just one instance now, is milling out of the wheat much, indeed most, of what the Creator put in to meet our bodily needs.

No nations are better fed than these two English-speaking nations. Yet, as a matter of mere sober fact, with loaded tables, our bodies are being hurt, crippled, starved, for lack of needed nourishment.

The Creator has put into the foods what our bodies need. We wash it out, or mill it out, or otherwise put or leave it out.

The physician may find our bodies ailing sorely for lack of some element the food we eat should give, but doesn't. It does not matter what you call it, if it actually supplies what is lacking.

It is clearly the particular kind of nourishment the body needs and isn't getting. The physician-expert, if he be wise enough, may help us live more in accord with the laws of our bodies commonly called the laws of health.

A simple striking incident is told of Leo Thirteenth. He was elected pope in his later sixties. He was very frail in health. It is said that he was finally elected after a long contest because it was thought he could not live long.

And then other plans could mature, and other ambitions among his electors could be achieved. So it was said. He outlived the entire College of Cardinals that elected him, finally dying in his ninety-fourth year, and remarkable for his intellectual vigour and his masterful grip on his policies to the end.

And he himself explained the human side of such a long life in spite of his extreme physical disabilities. He said he was not an expert in the knowledge of his body. He had a physician to advise him about the care of his body.

He followed faithfully the regimen of food, exercise, sleep and so on prescribed for him. Clearly he must have had a really wise skilled physician. And he attributed to this his remarkable mental vigour clear to the end of his unusually long life.

We may be disobeying flagrantly some law of our bodies. Obedience is the universal law of all life. There can't be health and vigour of body without intelligent obedience to its laws.

We are all fairly ignorant, for intelligent people really remarkably ignorant, in this regard. In the bodily emergency that has arisen there may be need of expert advice and guidance.

One at once remembers that this thoughtful intelligent obedience to the laws of the body is strictly in accord with God's general line of action. He loves nature's roads. He made them. They are sufficient for all common use.

We are supposed to use our thinking apparatus. Really, regeneration means a new *mental* birth as well as a new spirit birth.

But that's another story. Yet, be it keenly noted, in the emergency the supernatural swings into action. And life is full of emergencies.

I recall a friend in one of our leading Eastern cities. She was suffering severely at the time from some bodily ailment. She prayed repeatedly for healing, but it didn't come. And she wondered why. She was not conscious of any hindrance in her spirit life.

She had experienced healing by divine touch in answer to prayer more than once. She was

How Does Christ Heal?

in fellowship with a group of earnest saintly people who taught that the use of physician and means showed a lack of faith in Christ.

Puzzled, she went again to her knees in special prayer. As plain as could be the impression came, as distinct as a voice, to consult a certain physician. He was a Christian, who had formerly served in her family. And my impression is that he was sympathetic with the teaching of healing by Christ's direct touch.

There was a hesitancy about consulting a physician because of the teaching of the group of Christians with whom she was in fellowship. But that impression persisted, and was quite clear. She knew it was an answer, thus far, to her prayer.

She consulted the physician and in response to his questions told her story. He asked her what she ate. She said she could eat nothing but dry toast and tea. He told her these were poison to her body in its present condition.

He gave her no medicine, simply directions about food, and about the care of her body. She followed his expert advice, continued praying, and she quickly was quite well again.

Clearly enough she needed advice to help her obey intelligently the law of her body. Through the advice, and the obedience, and Christ's touch, the healing came. Ask Him. He'll tell you.

If one can imagine the supernatural healing touch given unwisely it is clear that it would confirm us in our ignorant or wilful disobedience to the law of our bodies.

Then another crisis comes, and another healing, and so on. Could anything be more abnormal? What a childish level of action! Instead Christ would lead us up to the level of intelligent mature action.

A friend, who bears an honoured name in earnest Christian circles, in one of our prominent cities, told me this simple bit out of her experience.

Her daughter, when a little baby, was suffering much from an earache, and crying piteously. The simple things she did for the child brought no relief.

Distressed in heart over her child's acute suffering she sent up a silent, earnest prayer for help. And she said to me, in her quiet, thoughtful way, that as clear as could be an inner voice said, "Put her feet in hot water."

The child's feet were hardly in the hot water when the crying ceased, a look of relief came into the dear little face, and the needed sleep had already come before the feet were dried.

The hot water drew the excess of blood away from the ear. Is it not a winsome bit in its sheer homeliness out of the Book of Life? How homely, in His sane, practical touch, is the blessed Holy Spirit.

Ask Christ. He'll be glad to tell you. But you must be careful to obey, simply, intelligently, fully. Failure to obey dulls the ears. You won't be so keen to hear next time He speaks.

I recall one time my back hurt me very much.

How Does Christ Heal? 87

The ache seemed always there. I knew I had been a sinner in the matter of overwork. But I had repented, and was trying to put my penitence into shoes. Still the nagging pain persisted.

I prayed for the healing touch. As clear as a bell, as quiet as the falling dew, the words were spoken into my inner ear, "Straighten up."

Years of travel, and of reading and writing on trains, had led to the habit of stooping. It was abnormal. My back was protesting. The vital organs within were being crowded. Pain is always a danger-signal, graciously warning us. At once I began straightening up, and I have been straightening up ever since. The pain quickly left.

The Holy Spirit is so practical. He's a real Friend. He wants to help. He helpeth our infirmities, of all sorts. Ask Christ. He'll tell you. And you'll hear if your ear is open, and your inner spirit quiet enough.

Do you remember the homely bit in the story of the healing of Hezekiah?[1] In answer to his pleading prayer Isaiah is sent with a message.

And this is part of what he said, "Take a cake of figs, and lay it for a plaster on the boil, and he will recover."

Then there was the supernatural shift backward of the shadow on the sun dial as an indication that God was actually at work on his behalf. What an exquisite blend of the homely

[1] 2 Kings 20:1-18. Isaiah 38:1-8, 21.

and the divine, the natural and the supernatural!

There was something Hezekiah's body needed that human hands could do. There was something else needed in his body that only God's touch could reach. The poultice did what it could. God's touch did what no poultice could have done. Both are used.

God loves nature's roads. But He unhesitatingly gives the more-than-natural touch when need be. Ask Him. He'll tell you. Then be sure you give Him the praise, as Hezekiah failed to do when his royal guest came from a far country.

One can understand that God moved the King of Babylon to come when he heard of Hezekiah's remarkable healing. Hezekiah failed God, and failed his visitor, too.

Sanity and Saintliness.

There's a fellowship of saintly Christian people who, among other blessed truths, teach healing by Christ's direct touch. Their testimony and activity have been graciously owned and used by God throughout the homeland and the foreign-mission world.

They insist that no means be used. It is a common word among them that to consult a physician and to use means reveal a lack of faith.

One is reluctant to say a word that even seems critical of such a saintly consecrated folk. Yet, clearly such condemnation of means is not according to the teaching of Scripture, nor the Holy Spirit's leading, nor God's general dealing with men, nor according to good sanctified common sense. The Holy Spirit's leading is the one touchstone of what to do.

It is striking that the most prominent false system of healing to-day, distinctly non-Christian, though using Christian phraseology, makes this same insistence on not using any material help of any sort. It is the one point of contact between two groups diametrically opposed at every other point.

One needs to avoid extremes. The sanity of the Holy Spirit awes. If one may say it with utmost reverence, the Holy Spirit is always so sane. There is no one so sane as the man actually under the control of the Holy Spirit. It's a touchstone. Saintliness and sanity naturally go together.

Faith Street is on the top of a hill. There are two roads slanting down on opposite sides, down to the lowlands and swamps.

On one side is Doubt Street. The slant down is scarcely noticeable at the first. It is so slight. And there are unseen traffic men always trying, by this means or that, to start you off that way, if ever so little at first.

On the opposite side of the hill is Queer Street. Its slant downward is almost none at all at the first. Still it's there.

Queer Street has a large number of one-room bungalows. So many personally lovely saintly people associate, all alone, each with himself, down there.

The only proper place to live is up on the top of the hill on Faith Street. The air is bracing there. Fogs and clouds are blown away.

Indeed some object that the air is too sharp. It's a searching air, they say. And then, they say, it's such a steep slant up to the top. It pulls your strength so, and takes your breath getting up.

But those who live there habitually talk much of the bracing quality of the atmosphere. The view is very clear, and far, and unobstructed. And there's a wondrous wind-harp on the top, whose soft rhythmic chordings refresh and strengthen.

Let us each one hire a moving van, if need be, and move up the steep slope to the top of the hill, and settle down up on Faith Street, and refuse to be budged down either way by the insistent traffic man.

It is interesting to notice that it is entirely possible to be both sane and saintly. No one is so sane as one actually swayed by the Holy Spirit in his mental processes, as well as in the habit of his life.

Keeping in touch with Christ through the Book, and the knees, and the habitual recognition of His presence, and keeping in touch with other humans, this keeps one wholesomely sane. It seasons both spirit and mental judgment.

Then, when any need arises, the first thing is

to ask Him, Christ, for the healing touch, and to ask Him what to do, if anything.

He guides us in the use of our common sense. The man surrendered in heart and will the Holy Spirit guides in thinking things through, and in knowing what to do.[1]

It ought to be the blessed commonplace that all bodily ailments, slight or serious, be prayed over the first thing.

I remember a gentle-faced young mother in the West, with two or three young children. She quietly said that as ailments arose with any of the children she always prayed with them, simply, briefly. And she knew, she said, what a practical difference it made.

If it's a serious case, perhaps a chronic case already in hand, the thing is to have a bit of quiet time alone with Christ over His book. Have a bit of getting in touch afresh.

Ask Christ. Wait quietly for His answer. Cultivate the quiet inner spirit. Ask expectantly, remembering that it is His first will to heal. He is willing to heal, and more is eager to heal. Reach out your hand and take all His Pierced Hand is reaching down to give.

A friend told me of having some trouble which seemed quite serious. She went to consult a physician in whom she had confidence, in a nearby city.

After a thorough examination he was quite sure she had cancer in her breast, and strongly advised an operation. There was then in ses-

[1] Psalm 25:9.

sion in the city a gathering of physicians and surgeons. A certain eminent surgeon was in attendance. Arrangements could be made for the operation by this specialist.

But there was a restraint within, my friend said, a restraint in her inner spirit, quite distinct. She did not agree. The physician deprecated delay, and plainly said it would be foolish not to do as he suggested, and at once. It was a peculiarly fortunate opportunity to have this visiting surgeon so immediately available, he said.

But the woman had prayed much before the consultation. The inner impression was clear. She returned home. And she prayed now with a clear knowledge of her serious need.

She asked definitely for Christ's healing touch. And she quietly told me that the lumps, and the sense of distress, gradually and completely left. This had been some years before. There had been no return of the trouble.

It was particularly interesting that she had no special contact at that time with those who taught healing. Many years before there had been such contact. As the trouble developed she remembered what she had heard long before.

And now without any special prayer with others, or conference, she simply pled the promise of the Book and asked for the healing, and it came. She is a thoughtful, quiet, earnest Christian woman, now past the prime of years, with no marked gift of leadership.

Another friend had the beginning of what

looked like cancer on her lower brow, plainly marked. The physician advised an operation, and feared that without it one eye would almost certainly be involved, and probably its sight lost. But she obeyed the inner restraint, not to have the operation.

My wife and I prayed with her, and later, at her request, I anointed her with oil, and again we prayed. The cancer never developed beyond the first stage noticed, and after the anointing it gradually and completely left. There is now no mark to be seen.

Recently a man whose home is in Texas told me of an experience of healing in his family. His six-year-old daughter had had a fever. It came up to the critical stage. The temperature was marked. The physician plainly revealed his anxiety, and feared that her strength would not be sufficient. It was doubted that she might survive the night. It was a time of sorest distress.

They were all worn out with the watching and nursing, day and night, and the concern of spirit. The child's weakness was such that the usual evening family prayers were held in the hallway with the child's room-door open.

At the child's own request a special prayer was made that Christ would heal her by His own direct touch. And the family were greatly touched and impressed with her simple, strong faith.

She said to her father in effect, "I'm going to be well now. Christ will heal me." She fell asleep with the words on her lips, and a smile on her wasted face. When the father and mother retired from the sick room one said to the other, "But suppose she isn't better in the morning; it'll be such a disappointment to her. What'll we do then?"

And the other replied, "But that isn't faith. Faith believes it will be as we asked." In the morning the child awoke with her temperature quite normal, and speedily recovered her strength.

Let us live in simple, full touch of life with our living Christ. And when any need may come go to Him. It is His eager will to advise with us, and above all to heal us, to His glory.

For those we touch will know what a Christ Christ is. It will let them see His glory, that is, see the sort of a Saviour He is.

V

HOW FAR MAY CHRIST'S HEALING BE EXPECTED? CHRIST'S GIVING AND MAN'S TAKING

It is Christ's will that we be pure in heart, intelligent in understanding, well balanced in judgment, in the grip of a noble purpose, flamed by a strong passion, strong and well in body, and in that touch of heart and understanding with Himself where we can reach out and take all His Pierced Hand is now reaching down to give.

Healed but Limping.

How far may Christ's power be expected to meet our bodily needs? We commonly say that there is no limit to His power to meet our spiritual needs. Is there a limit in our bodily needs?

There is, of course, no limit to Christ's *power*. It seems to be a matter of His *willingness*, what He thinks it is best or wisest to do for us in this regard.

There's such a wide range of bodily ailments. It runs from a nervous headache to organic heart trouble. It may be a crick in your back or a chronic lameness, or anywhere in between.

Troubles that come from disturbed nervous conditions are more quickly affected by a changed mental attitude. Functional troubles are reckoned more susceptible to treatment than organic. Indeed organic troubles are usually quite ruled out.

A nervous condition may bring on a serious palpitation of your heart. The right touch on the nerves would make the heart's beating all right again.

Some troubles are commonly classed as distinctly outside the range of healing, whether some system of mental suggestion, or Christ's own supernatural touch of power.

I recall running across a certain man in a Western city. He was well known in Christian circles as a leader in city mission work in New York City.

He had made the journey west to get in touch with a Christian teacher of healing. And he told me that he had been healed of a rather serious trouble.

But he had been lame for many years. And as we parted he limped away. I looked after him. He was praising Christ for the healing of his body.

But it had never occurred to him that this serious chronic lameness might have been healed too, nor apparently to the man who prayed with him. Was he right? Is there a limit in this regard?

There is nothing commoner than the use of eye-glasses to help defective or weak eyes. It is common among many who teach healing, the mental sort alone, and the Christ supernatural sort of healing.

How Far May Healing Be Expected 97

One listens to eager, joyous voices praising God for the healing touch that has come, perhaps to some remarkably radical extent.

But the eye-glasses are there. It seems a bit puzzling. Is there a limit to the power we may expect?

There can be no question that the eyes are vitally connected with one's health and vigour. Eye-strain has been responsible for serious nervous troubles, and for many a nervous breakdown. It's an intensely practical question so far as health is concerned.

The eyes are affected much by nervous conditions. The use of glasses adapted to certain inaccuracies in the eyes, of course, tends to confirm and harden those inaccuracies.

It is being insisted upon in certain eye-specialist circles that a proper nervous relaxation will actually correct practically all eye inaccuracies. And this new teaching is having a wide acceptance and application abroad, as well as here.

Our next Talk lays much emphasis on a right mental attitude. A simple childlike trust in Christ affects one's habitual mental attitude.

And this in turn has an influence on all bodily conditions quite beyond what we can take in.

Sometimes aged persons will have what is spoken of as "second sight." I do not mean now the psychical sense of seeing into the future, and that sort of thing, which is spoken of in this same way.

But there is a physical "second sight" referred to. It is not uncommon to find one in the seventies or later who has laid aside eyeglasses entirely, and is able to see and to read easily without their aid.

Is it possible that this is simply such a relaxation of the nerves as normalizes the eyes again?

Is it possible that the habitual spirit of unquestioning faith in Christ, and so the habitual right attitude of mind, would so affect our bodies, and our nerves as to include our eyes?

Beyond this, may we pray expectantly for the healing touch on our eyes? The relation of the question to one's health is clear enough. It is a matter of health, vitally. What should we expect? How much?

One's teeth have a still closer relation to health. The remarks about Christians undoubtedly experiencing healing, and yet having faulty eyes, could be repeated about the teeth, as extensively, maybe more.

Modern dentistry certainly is having a large field of activity, and ever increasing. That it has gone through many experimental stages, and isn't out of them yet, is of course a commonplace.

And the experimenting is always at human expense of suffering and ill health. Many of the things said about the medical profession, as regards commercialism, the rapid wholesaling process, the blundering personal equation, and the like, could be repeated here.

Without question dentistry is a science and

How Far May Healing Be Expected 99

art combined, mechanical art and artistic art. And without doubt untold numbers have been distinctly helped.

Of course, food affects the teeth very much, the sort of food. This is particularly true of growing children, and of expectant mothers and nursing mothers.

The commercialism and the cookery that takes out of the food certain substances needed to build up bones and teeth, make for deficient and defective teeth. So does the unbalanced diet.

Such teeth easily break down and give out in the grind of daily use. Of course, obedience to nature's laws here means the proper cleansing and care of the teeth from childhood up.

Even with the best that the most skilled conscientious dentist can do, substitute teeth are so much less than the natural that no comparison can be made.

The two things are too far apart for comparison. Loss of natural teeth lessens health and vigour and length of life, regardless of the dentist's utmost skill.

Does dentistry simply give a maimed man a pair of crutches so he can hobble along somehow, instead of not at all?

Is it simply good for those who don't and won't come to Christ for what He has to give? Or is there more? How much may we properly, sanely expect, and not be disappointed?

The Need the Measure of Power.

It becomes of intense interest to turn back and

note the extent of Christ's healing in the Gospel days.

The list of healings there has a few acute cases, but most of them are the absolutely incurable incorrigibles. A man blind from birth is included, with the possibility that the eyeballs were not fully matured or developed.

One summary actually says that the maimed were made whole. There is only one meaning when that word "maimed" is used, whether the Greek or English word is examined. And that is, that a limb or arm or foot, or some other part, that had been lost was replaced by a new one.

That would be distinctly creative power at work. But the meaning of the language used is quite beyond question.

And then the last word in extremes is said in the raising of the dead, even Lazarus dead four days.

And the same sort of thing is repeated in the Acts. The beggar man in Jerusalem at the gate of the temple had been lame from birth. Now he leaps up, and walks. There's an abundance of strength, where there had been none at all.

The Lystra man had never walked. And, even here, there are the two dead raised. There's Dorcas near the beginning of the Acts, and there is the Troas young man toward the end, when some might think of the extent of power as possibly waning.

There can be no question about how far healing was actually experienced in these early days.

The need was the measure of the power. The seriousness of the case didn't affect the power available.

There were degrees of disability. But there were no degrees in the power at Christ's command, and in response to the disciples' Spirit-led actions.

The power was always abundant, not scanty. The power was sufficient for the worst case. But what about now? How far may healing be expected to-day? Up to the limit of real need?

It seems like a very difficult question, at first flush, unless indeed it is answered at once by some with a positive negative.

Yet, there's an answer. And it is an answer that really answers. It is not a piously rhetorical evasion.

Ask Christ.

There are two parts to the answer. The first is this: *ask Christ.* You can come into the simple touch with Him where you can ask, and He will answer your question, and answer it fully.

That's an enormous advantage, to get actually in touch with the Christ that has all power, and has used it in this way.

Recall, if you will, what was said in our last Talk about getting into touch with Christ.

Ask Christ. He has the power to. That is clear. He did have the love to when He was down here. That's clear, too.

He thought it the wise thing to loosen out His

power through His followers in those early sample Church days.

Ask Christ about your own need, whatever it may be. He is there at your side. He is intensely interested. He will answer your question.

Each one of us is a door. We are Christ's door, or we may be. We are His door into the whole circle where we live.

He wants to get through us to them. His dealings with us are an acted-out plea to them. Through these He talks to them.

The freer hand He can have with us the more He can touch them through us. We should eagerly yet patiently get into the sort of touch where He *can* give all He wants to. That means all we need.

Perhaps you're in that school we are to talk about soon. You need to learn a thing or two, maybe.

The thing we're needing may be withheld because there's something we're needing more. We may not know about that other need.

It may mean a radical face-about to know about that other thing, and more radical yet to be willing to get it, with all it involves.

Maybe you've got a term in school before you can get all you're needing. But then you can make it a very short term, if you will.

And, *and*, the Devil may be hindering. There is no bit of teaching more bitterly hated, and more stubbornly fought against, than this of bodily healing by Christ's supernatural touch.

Those who are in a place of leadership, or who have the personal gift of leadership, are yet more bitterly opposed than those otherwise placed or gifted.

One has to insist through bitter opposition often. The thing is to be clear of the Holy Spirit's leading, and then insist on having all He has for you.

Ask Christ your question. And remember, as you ask, about His *first* will for us. It includes whatever is included in this: full bodily health and vigour, to His glory. That's the first half of the answer.

God's Giving: Our Taking.

The second part goes a little deeper in. It is this: Christ's *giving* is dependent on our *taking*. You can't give into a tight shut fist. Christ can't.

There's a striking little word on Christ's lips in that Betrayal Night Talk.[1] He and the inner group are walking under the full moon, past the Herod temple with its beautiful brass grape-vine.

Christ says, "Ye did not choose me, but I chose you." They did choose Him as a Saviour. He chose them for the bit of service they were to do.

"And appointed you," He goes on, "that ye should go and bear fruit." The fruit was the life, what they really were in themselves. All service roots down in the life.

[1] John 15:16.

"And that your fruit shall abide." Not green, gnarly fruit, but full-grown, luscious, juicy fruit. He means us to live a life matured and ripened in its spiritual experiences.

"That whatsoever ye shall ask." Note that: prayer, like service, grows out of the life. The life in touch prays, and can pray, and can pray the prayer that loosens out Christ's power *to the full*.

"Whatsoever ye shall ask the Father in my name, He *may* give it you." The striking word is that word "may."

It is not *shall* this time, but *may*. Every other time the word used in this connection is shall; this time it is may.

"Shall" means His willingness to do, His purpose. "May" means our coöperation with Him. "Shall" is His side, "may" is ours.

Our asking makes it possible for God to give. We give Him the open channel. God needs an open hand, and that means an open life.

Christ's giving is always dependent on our taking. And we are such beggarly takers. No human hand has ever yet reached up to take as much as Christ's pierced hand is reaching down to give.

For the taking must be on a level with the giving. It means that touch where we want what He wants. He leads us. We follow.

We talk much about God's sovereignty, without understanding much about just what it means. We don't talk so much about man's sovereignty.

How Far May Healing Be Expected

Practically, God's sovereignty means that ultimately, through the tangled-up network of human wills, God's love-plan for things down here will work fully out. Yet it will be without infringing on any man's free choice and action.

Man's sovereignty, as planned by God, means that everything we have and get and do is through our own choice.

God's sovereignty waits on man's sovereignty, His purposes on our glad coöperation. And some day these two will run side by side. And man's sovereignty will be deliberately merged in God's. His love will win our choice.

But, just now, the bit to emphasize is this: in actual life the biggest thing is man's taking. We may have, out of Christ's down-stretched hand, all we *can* take, and then all we actually *will* take, and *do* take.

It's a three-sided transaction. Christ reaches down to give all we need, without any limit or restriction. We reach up and take out of His hand.

The Devil reaches over to keep us from taking out of Christ's hand. He tries to keep our hands, Christ's hand and mine, out of touch, if possible.

He befogs the air so we don't see straight in our reaching. He tries to teeter our reaching hands, this way and that, or to make them not reach up far enough so as to touch.

He does his best to tire us, to wear us out, so we'll quit the reaching. When he slips here he starts in afresh over there.

The Limit of Our Consent.

There's a remarkable bit from Paul's pen that fits in here. It says that all power needed by any one (in touch with Christ) is already within himself.

It is a matter of letting this power that is within actually meet the need. The need you feel so keenly and the power to meet that need, are close neighbours. You have both. It's a matter of the two getting together.

The passage is in the little letter to the Ephesian church, where Paul had that two-years' remarkable healing ministry. It becomes the more striking because the particular thing being talked about in this letter is this: the power of God *at our disposal* to meet our need.

There's a threefold standard or measure of that power, the raising of Christ when He was dead,[1] the making of a new man inside one dead in sin,[2] and the changing bitterest enemies into dearest friends.[3] Pretty high standard of power that could do such things!

Paul says we may expect *that* power, which is now within us, to meet any need for us to-day up to that measure or limit. That covers what we are talking about just now, and more.

The striking bit comes at the end of chapter three.[4] In simple language here is what Paul is saying, in part. The Holy Spirit is power.

[1] Ephesians 1: 18–22.
[2] Ephesians 2: 1–10.
[3] Ephesians 2: 11–22.
[4] Ephesians 3: 16–20.

He in Himself is all the power of God. He is now inside each of us. He comes in through the opened door of our faith. He reproduces Christ's own character in us, so far as we let Him have sway.

The big thing He does is to fill our hearts with that tender, strong passion, the love of Christ. This comes to include every other needed trait of character.

Then Paul sums up all in this: "Unto Him who is able to do exceeding abundantly above all we ask or think, according to the power that worketh in us——"

That is to say, He is able to do, not simply what we ask, but what we are *thinking* about that we wish He would do.

Then Paul piles things up in a rare way. He is able to do *above* that, then *abundantly* above that, then *exceeding* abundantly above that. That is a tremendous climax.

And the one outstanding characteristic of this power is *love*. It is a power of love. He can and He will. Love controls the power. That surely answers our question.

And then the measure or the limit or the extent, up to which we may expect this power is put in these words, "*according to the power that worketh in us.*" That means up to the measure of that power working in us.

Of course, the power itself is without any limit. But the Holy Spirit always works with our consent. He does only as much as we let Him do. Everything He does is as we are willing. So the limit of the working is *the limit of our consent.* He'll do all we let Him.

As we let Him work *in* us all He wants to, He works *for* us all we need. If we let Him work character *in* us (Christ's character) He's free to work bodily healing *for* us.

We let Him work out His fruit *in* us, love, joy, peace, yes, long-suffering, gentleness, goodness, meekness, faithfulness, self-mastery. Then He is free to work out *for* us the healing our bodies need, and our circumstances, too.

Fruit-growing is a gradual thing, seed-sowing, pruning, sun and rain, dew and air, spraying for hurtful insects, then bud and blossom, the beginning of the fruit, and its gradual growth up to juicy, luscious, full-sized fruit. It's a gradual thing. All growth is. One must be patient and steady, very steady. But sometimes it is surprisingly quick when it is the fruit the Holy Spirit bears in the soil of our character.

Nine Things About Taking.

How far may we expect Christ's healing? The answer is this: we *may* have all we *can* take. And then all we *do* take.

But please notice a few simple yet radical things about the taking. They've been spoken of partly before in another connection.

The taking must be in Christ's Name, pleading His blood. The Devil yields only to whom he must. And he must to Christ.

The taking must be by one in actual touch of

heart with Christ. The Devil laughs at any one else.

The taking must be in the utmost humility. Our sins cost Christ so much suffering, and this that we take has been bought for us with His blood.

The taking must be definite. The Devil yields only *what* he must. The taking must be persistent. The Devil yields only *when* he must. And he's a sly, deceitful, toughened fighter by strategy as well as by ugly force.

The taking must be as the Holy Spirit guides. The touchstone of all prayer is the Holy Spirit's guidance. He puts the prayer to be prayed into one's heart.

No mere asking for something because of some one else's experience will do. That experience may be blessed. But there must be one's own direct leading, over the open Book, on the bent knee.

The taking must be *with the life*. No mere church membership, and activity and giving, and the like, will do.

No simple taking of the sacred bread and the holy cup will answer here. These may all be very blessed.

But the taking must be with the very life. And it is so. One finds that it is only the life actually lived for Christ, by His grace, that can reach up and take to the full what His blood has redeemed.

And, then, will you keenly mark, that you take only as much as you *can* take. The power to take varies with various persons, and even at various times with the same person. It all depends on one's personal touch with Christ.

And you take only as much as you actually *do* take. As a rule, the conception of *how much* you may take varies. It varies with circumstances and with one's mood. The Spirit's leading is the decisive thing.

But, *but,* it is Christ's first will that we shall be made strong and well in our bodies *up to the limit of our need.*

And He is by your side now eagerly waiting to give. Giving won't make Him any poorer, only gladder.

I have the privilege, which I prize highly, of the friendship of Mr. James Moore Hickson, the consecrated, talented, Church-of-England layman of London.

Christ has been using him in a remarkable healing ministry of recent years throughout the six continents. Our friendship runs back over many years on both sides the Atlantic.

One day I asked him to tell me the most notable instances of healing of which he knew personally. And he told me of two that I want to relate here.

Mr. Hickson had gone to visit a woman in her home in the Midlands in England. She had been bedridden for years with rheumatoid arthritis.

That disease, it will be remembered, affects the joints of the body. In this case the joints were

How Far May Healing Be Expected 111

locked up or rigid. The woman had not been able to move herself for several years.

Mr. Hickson prayed for her healing. That evening she moved herself, the first time in years.

Her husband wrote that the next morning she rose from the bed, dressed herself, and went about the house, as in the earlier years.

That was the first of these two experiences. That disease is classed as incurable.

The second incident was of a young boy of twelve years or so, with a club-foot, from his birth.

He was brought to the church where a healing mission was being conducted. He came up to the front of the church with his attendant, wearing an iron brace to help him in walking.

As Mr. Hickson saw the boy in front of him, and with one quick glance took in the situation, he said to himself involuntarily, "Oh! this is a *deformity!*"

His thought was that this was not a disease, but presented a much different, and much more difficult, case to handle.

In telling me the story Mr. Hickson said that instantly that quiet inner voice said, "Who is doing this? You or I?"

And he said in his heart, "Forgive me, Lord," and aloud he said to the attendant, "Take off the irons."

He took the boy's foot in his hands and made a simple bit of prayer, as is his custom.

The next day the boy was brought again. There was some improvement marked in the foot. Again he prayed, and the boy's foot gradually became quite normal, and he wore an ordinary shoe.

How far may Christ's healing be expected? We may have all we can take, as His Spirit guides our taking.

Thou blessed Christ, thou solitary God-Man, who didst live a full life of human experience, and then didst die as none other did nor could nor can,

And then didst live again, and still livest, and some day wilt finish up the racial end of Thine earth task,

Help me now to reach out and up and take out of Thy Pierced Hand all Thou hast for me, to Thy glory among my fellows.

I ask it on the ground of Thy blood shed for me, and Thy Word pledged to me. Amen.

VI

THE HUMAN SIDE OF HEALING AND HEALTH

It is Christ's will that we be pure in heart and motive and life, truly human in character up to the level of His humanness, fired by a noble passion, in the grip of a worthy purpose, in warm touch with Himself and with our fellows, and strong and vigorous in all our bodily functions.

Health? or Healing.

HEALTH is more than healing. There's more of it. It calls for more of the Creator's power. It means more to a man. And it will be the means of greater spiritual blessing if things are as they were meant to be.

The task of keeping men in health, even as much health as they have, is immeasurably greater than healing all who need healing, even if they would all come for healing.

Christ is greatest in the unrecognized power He is expending on men all the time. And all this power has the Calvary mark upon it. It is all red-tinged.

Health means rhythm, the smooth working of all parts together. Disease is a break in the rhythm. Rhythm is ease. A break in the rhythm means absence of ease, dis-ease, of some sort.

114   About the Healing Christ!

When there's full rhythm within your body, and with your fellows, and with Christ, and with nature, there's fulness of life flowing in and flooding out.

But, *but*, there's a break, a bad break in the rhythm of life, within and without and above. Within we call it disease, without friction and strife, strikes and war. Above we call it sin.

But, in spite of the break, Christ continues His touch of creative power on all life, giving health and strength. This becomes less as we hinder.

There is full life only as we let Him do and give all He wants to. There's the added touch, giving healing, where the way is open to Him for that.

The first is the natural thing, the second is supernatural in addition to the natural. The first is for all, the second is for those needing it and who will come where He can give it.

There's one thing better than being healed. And this is being *kept in health*. Then healing isn't needed. It's the higher level, higher in intelligence and maturity of character.

It is higher in obedience, and in the taking from Christ's hand, day by day, all we need. And it costs Christ more in the continual giving out of power.

Christ's creative power through natural channels is commonplace, blessedly commonplace. It is everywhere. It is in every one, without exception.

His supernatural power is exceptional.

Where His natural power is allowed freest hand there is less need of the supernatural.

But that break of sin is so sore, and so much in evidence everywhere, that there is a constant need of the supernatural.

And there would be far more of the supernatural if the way were open. For Christ will do anything and everything to overcome the break of sin. He came that we might have life, and have it in uncommon measure.

There is the divine side of health and healing, and there is the human side. The two intermingle so continually that it's difficult to talk about the one without touching on the other.

But, just now, we want to talk a little about the human side. There's so much need of simple, clear teaching.

Living in that touch with Christ's natural laws of life, and in the direct touch with Himself, where health is the common thing, and healing is not needed, this, *this*, is the higher, the highest level of living.

It is striking to find two distinct trails in the Old Testament, a healing trail and a health trail. The two run side by side.

And it is of intense interest to find the health trail greater in the space it takes up, and in the emphasis laid upon it.

It is the more interesting because this little Hebrew nation becomes a model of life *in the ideals* taught and insisted upon.

We traced partially, in an earlier Talk,[1] the

[1] "Is It Christ's Will to Heal Our Bodies To-day?"

healing trail in the Old Testament. It was a trail of teaching and of healing.

There is the plain teaching that God would heal. And it is used as a plea to pull them up to the higher level. And there is the string of incidents where men were actually healed in a positive supernatural way.

The Jew Health Trail.

Now, side by side with that, goes this other trail, longer, broader, more marked. It is a teaching about health. There is a remarkable course in personal hygiene here. Instruction is given repeatedly, and obedience is insisted upon.

Some of these items may seem very homely and commonplace. But it is careful attention and obedience to detail that makes perfection in anything.

Nothing is too common or commonplace if its practice means physical vigour. And physical vigour affects mental alertness and spiritual attainment.

There is particular stress laid upon *food*. Pains are taken to specify the things they must not eat.[1] And Moses repeats this in much detail in that last series of Quiet Talks in the Plains of Moab.[2] This would cultivate a thoughtfulness about food.

Without any question there is a hygienic principle underlying all these instructions and re-

[1] Leviticus 11: 1-23..
[2] Deuteronomy 14: 3-21.

strictions. They were an agricultural people, with small exporting facilities, and so the fruits of trees and soil would naturally bulk big in their daily food.

Then the item of *physical exercise* had a big place. There was plenty of work to be done, in connection with cultivation of fields, orchards, vineyards, and common gardening.

It was a common custom that every Hebrew had some fixed occupation. And every one shared in the daily tasks indoors and out.

The ideal communities that have sprung up here and there, where all share in all tasks, have their truest highest ideal actually practised among these pastoral agricultural Hebrews.

And one is keen to note the other side of this. There was particular attention given to *rest*, relaxation. There is a rare poise between work and rest aimed at here.

There are four distinct items in the rest or relaxation program, which Moses was careful to mark out for them, at God's direction.

One day in seven was to be kept, sacred from toil, sacred to rest of body. The emphasis upon this is marked and continuous.

Three times a year there were special times of relaxation from their usual occupation, the Passover, the Feast of the First-fruits, and the Harvest-home Festival. Each was for seven days.

The men were to go up to Jerusalem to these feasts. Including travel it must have meant a ten-days' relaxation for most of them, with an absorbing objective.

Every seven years the land must lie fallow. Modern farmers might well note this. The land enriched itself. The land rested, and of course the people rested.

There would be much to attend to, but there was a break in the work schedule. It meant the rest and relaxation of a change.

Every fiftieth year was the time of special jubilation, following the plan of the seventh year. The average man would be likely to go through, at least, two of these jubilee years.

Then, of course, in common with all men, every day had its night. There was the daily alternation of rest and work. And nature itself provides for more sleep in winter and less in summer. A simple pastoral folk follows nature more closely.

So, all told, there were six items in the common Hebrew rest or relaxation program, a day of sleep for every day's work, and a longer time of nightly sleep for half the year.

Then there was one day in seven, three special times each year, one year in seven, and an extra year in every fifty years.

Rather a remarkable program that. Yet the fact of its being provided by Moses, at God's direction, is immensely suggestive.

Physical exercise, and time for the mind to store up and meditate, time for social recreation and enjoyment, time for worship, all this becomes of greatest interest from *the health point of view.*

And particular directions were given about *the ablutions,* the frequent all-over bathing by the priests. And the priests were the practical rulers of the people.

The priesthood was the fixed system of national administration through the centuries. They were the leaders. And what the leaders do the people do. Like priest like people.

There were special directions for special bathing in connection with their sanitary and quarantine codes. They were a bathing people. Cleanliness of person was a fixed habit.

There were careful community *sanitation* regulations covering the individual tents and the whole encampment in the Wilderness, and afterward when settled in Canaan.

The *quarantine* regulations were explicit and rigid, inspection by experts, isolation, and segregation. The strictest watch was constantly kept on the people's health, on all suspicious cases, and on the diseased. Quarantine is worthless unless rigid, and rigidly enforced. Their ideals have never been improved upon.

And, of course, their inflexible law of *circumcision* was rooted down in the physical. Apart from other significance it was a hygienic regulation. It belonged in their scheme of cleanliness and provision against infection.

Now, note keenly, that the Hebrews were essentially *an out-of-doors people*. They lived in God's open air.

There were the four hundred years in Egypt. Egypt was an open air country characteristically, and is to this day. The absence of rain, the dryness of the air, and its rare tonic qualities, were marked features, and are. The open air habit had a good start in Egypt.

The forty years in the Wilderness sands simply meant forty years in the open air. Quite likely most of them slept out in the open.

Moses himself was habituated to this open air life through his sheep-tending years in Midian, as well as his earlier Egypt years, and later Wilderness years.

And there's one more item worth mentioning in this health memorandum. Their *land laws*, their scheme of inheritance, the reversion of land to the original owner every fifty years which entered into all sales and transfers, these, of course, would tend to contentment of mind regarding the future. Fear of the future, mostly groundless, makes a shorter road to the graveyard.

Here are eight items in their national health program to which they were habituated through the centuries. It included food, work or exercise, rest and relaxation and play, personal cleanliness, community sanitary measures, quarantine against disease, open air living, and a measure of contentment about the future, the rainy day.

This is the health trail that runs all through these Old Testament pages, and clearly ran all through the physical life of this remarkable race of people.

Without doubt it plays a large part in attempting to explain the astonishing physical vigour of the Jews even to-day.

Inheritance persists. They have suffered persecutions, hardships, privations, that would have killed off any ordinary people. Plainly they are not ordinary people. Their health program certainly was not ordinary. It was rather extraordinary. What nation to-day can come near it?

This is the health trail running side by side with that blessed healing trail. It persists through these old pages. It puts a remarkable emphasis on the human side of health and healing.

It was planned by God. It surely becomes a personal model for the thoughtful man to-day, and especially the thoughtful Christian man.

The Eden Health Model.

Now, there's another model of life in these older pages. The Hebrew nation, as planned by God, gives one model. Here's another. It's yet earlier. It comes in before the break of sin had set things so askew.

It's the model of the true full human, the human as yet unhurt by sin. It's the Adam-and-Eve-in-Eden model.

It is really God's ideal of human life. And it is put here at the very first where any one can quickly see it.

Of course, I am a little old-fashioned about man's start on this earth. This other teaching has so befogged all the air that it's quite refreshing to turn back to God's own picture. I am rather fond of some old-fashioned things, water, open air, fresh fruit, natural wheat, the Bible, and the like.

Adam was made the true full normal human, by direct act of God. He stood at the highest point of mature manhood, physically, mentally, and in spirit understanding.

He knew civilization at its highest, in miniature. For civilization does not consist in the culture which the Greeks had, nor the highly organized life of the Roman, nor the organized complexity of modern times.

Civilization is a moral thing. Civilization means harmonious life in contact with others. And the essential thing there is moral ideals and moral conduct. So far as any civilization lacks these it is less than real civilization.

Look at God's picture, His model in Eden. It is simple, delightfully simple, but never crude, and certainly not savage.

Here is a human, fresh from the hand of God. He is on terms of intimacy with God. They talk and walk and are busily occupied with their work together.

This man has an intimate congenial human friend at his side sharing all his life. He has a daily occupation, caring for a garden.

He has before him a great inspiring task, subduing the whole earth. There's the immediate and the distant, the near and the far, something for hands and something for mind.

He lived in the open air, sleeping as well as working and resting there. The second day he lived was marked as a rest day.

Human Side of Healing

He had a daily task, work and exercise combined. He had a fruit diet. His food was all sun-cooked. He had pure water to drink. There was running water to bathe in.

Is it not a winsome picture? One is more than ever insistent on getting away from the modern phrase "the ascent of man," and toward the older phrase "the descent of man."

Certainly it would be a going *up* to go back to that old Eden standard of civilization and culture and life.

And there is a plain intimation, too, that this first man's bodily vigour hinged on his keeping in touch with his friendly Companion, God.

Do you remember that day they are standing under that tree of opportunity? Through choosing not to eat of it as God wished him not to do, choosing to choose God's choice, Adam would be stepping into a still closer intimacy with God. The highest thing can come only through choice.

There is a gentle but very plain word of warning about that tree. He *could* misuse the opportunity it gave him. He *could* break friendship with God if he chose.

And this is the word of warning, "For in the day that thou eatest thereof, dying, thou shalt die."[1] The dying would come automatically through the break.

There would be a beginning, a continued process, and a final result. The moment he ate was the beginning. The process went on for

[1] Genesis 2:17, paraphrase.

years. The actual bodily death didn't come till long years after.

Now, that intimation naturally includes the reverse, *i. e.*, if thou keep in touch with me, by thine own voluntary choice, *living, thou shalt live.*

There would be the same movement in the opposite direction, a beginning, a process, a final result. Choosing God's way would bring him yet closer to God.

That would be the beginning of a new life by his own choice. And that would grow from less to more until a fulness of life would come, such as one simply can't take in.

Touch with God is the basis of full life, bodily, mental, of the spirit. The other word for touch is obedience.

Obedience is a music word. It means the rhythm of God's will and a man's will. No sweeter music was ever made on earth, or heard in heaven.

All this, you notice, has to do simply with the human side of health. This early model gives God's own thought of the true full natural human man, as He planned him.

This Eden idea says, in effect, that a man should have a noble passion, a human friend, a daily task, and an outreaching purpose that calls for all there is in him.

His immediate bodily needs are open air, simple food, the exercise of a daily task, a time of rest, and running water near by.

This first man's passion was for his Friend,

to please Him. To carry out His plan. By his side was his complemental self, his one nearest human friend with whom all his life was shared.

There was a garden of trees and flowers and all growing things to care for, and the cultivation of the whole earth entrusted to him to think about and plan for.

The Christian and the True Human.

Now, will you notice keenly that the Christian life means simply the true human life? Sin made the break. Christ mends the break. He renews and restores man. The natural thing native to a man's being is this of living the true, full, Christian life.

Anything that isn't really Christian isn't human. It's lower down. It's less, or a bad more, or a distortion. Sin, selfishness, are lower down than the human level. They hurt the true human. They hurt our health and strength.

The true Christian life is the real key to health, and to healing where healing is needed. The emphasis, of course, is on that word "true."

We are so used to the cheapened, thinned-out meanings, being "saved" from hell and into heaven, church membership, with some attendance, some giving of money and maybe service, more or less, as happens to suit one's ideas; this seems the sum total ofttimes.

It's a sort of insurance policy. The chief thing is keeping up the premiums. It's a sort of immunity bath, a quarantine measure. Sometimes it is the ticket of admission into certain social circles. So much Christianity has no ethical quality to it. It never hurts anybody's conscience, nor changes his habits.

Of course, in the simple, true meaning the Christian life is a tender passion burning deep, and then deeper. It's a purpose gripping all one's powers.

It means on the inner side spirit fellowship with the Man that died, on the outer side a warm upright human touch with one's fellows.

It means the Jesus passion in control. It is very simple. Some of the simplest unlettered homeliest folks, as well as some of the most scholarly and cultured, quite understand all this. They live it.

Christ enriches everything He touches. The Devil vulgarizes everything he can lay his hands on. Christ makes the commonest thing hallowed. The Devil makes the purest, the hallowed things, vulgarly common and cheap.

The Devil puts the devilish touch into man's life, sometimes foul, sometimes cultured, always devilish. Christ restores the hurt human up to the true human level. Calvary neutralizes the Devil's power, and restores and enriches the Eden ideal. The new Eden has the passion of sacrificial love in it.

Now, it is of the simple real Christian life that I am thinking when I say this: the Christian life is the key to health and to healing. This is the human side of both.

One's Mental Attitude.

There are *two things* that will grow up in such a simple, true, Christian life. They are simple things, but they lie at the very foundation.

They are, a right mental attitude, and an intelligent obedience to the laws of health. And these are the two things to be emphasized in this Quiet Talk.

Let us talk first about that *right mental attitude.* I do not mean that you are to try to have a right mental attitude, simply. That becomes incidental. The emphasis is on something else. That attitude comes naturally out of that something else.

I mean this: you think about Christ. He died for you. He has won the love of your heart. You trust Him.

You believe Him. You accept what He says in the Book. You follow where He plainly leads. All this is what faith is. It is thinking about Him.

You get filled up with *Him,* who He is, how He loved and loves, what He did, His plans for you, and His promises to you.

You are full of this, that He is living to-day. He is all absorbed with things down here. He's intensely interested in you, with personal solicitude for your personal need, and with a plan for your life.

This is what faith means; not thinking about your faith, thinking about *Him.* It isn't looking *in;* it's looking *up*—to *Him.*

Now, once that gets fixed in some measure, as a habit, a growing habit, it will affect your mental attitude.

Your plans and problems, your difficulties and perplexities, your personal habits and temptation, all will instinctively be affected by this mental attitude.

Christ will loom up in your mind practically as the biggest thing in all your life. You will get into the habit of connecting everything with Him. And *that mental attitude will vitally and radically affect your body.*

The worst enemy we all have (outside of the Devil himself) is fear. I mean the fear that is a dread of something.

There are three kinds of fear. The fear of reverence grows out of love, and is good. The fear of caution grows out of the presence or possibility of danger, and is only good.

The fear that is afraid of something or some one, a dread, a slavish fear, is bad, only bad, and is a positive injury to one's body.

It may grow out of ignorance. Often it is a result of overwrought nerves. It exerts an incalculable influence on one's bodily condition. It controls the imagination, and the imagination controls the body.

All diseases and bodily ailments of whatever sort fall into three groups. Those that are imaginary; they have no existence at all except in imagination.

Then there are those ailments which are the result of the imagination's influence on the body. And then there are ailments originating otherwise.

It will seem astonishing if I say that a very large proportion of all bodily ailments is above the ears, or have their origin there, that is, in the imagination. And the smaller proportion is below the ears.

This seems astonishing. It may be honestly questioned by those not familiar with the subject. But increased observation only tends to confirm the truth of the statement.

Job says, "I feared a fear and it came upon me."[1] His sense of dread acted so on his imagination that it actually produced in his body the thing he feared.

The Power of Fear.

Only a little thinking will remind any one that fear, the slavish fear that dreads, is inbred in most people.

From the cradle up, the whip of fear is the commonest thing known. This fear is instilled, unconsciously, unintentionally, ignorantly, habitually, from earliest years on through school life and long after.

It is inbred further by the very evil abnormal atmosphere of our surroundings. It becomes a habit of mind. And the actual bodily injury done is quite beyond calculation.

An illustration that has become notable of this sort of thing is the story of the man condemned

[1] Job 3:25—free reading.

130   About the Healing Christ

to death for murder. A group of physicians proposed an experiment as a matter of scientific research. The civil authorities concerned agreed.

They proposed to the condemned man that he submit to a serious surgical operation. And if he survived his sentence of death would be remitted and he allowed to go free. He agreed.

He was stretched on the operating table, face down. A thin bit of cold steel was slowly drawn across his back as though a knife cutting.

At the same time it was arranged that water would drip from his back, drop by drop, steadily down, so it could easily be heard.

The physicians talked together in his hearing, giving the impression that he was bleeding from a wound, and would certainly bleed to death.

The man actually expired. Yet his body had not been touched except as described. I am not defending the deceit used.

It is a striking illustration of the slavery of the body to the imagination. He imagined he was surely bleeding to death. And the imagination actually brought death. He feared a fear and it came upon him.

I recall a mother whose baby was ill. The mother's milk didn't agree, but seemed to nauseate. The mother had been a trained nurse. She is an earnest Christian woman.

But certain very difficult circumstances that touched her very closely had embittered her spirit extremely. As she thought into things prayerfully she was led to see just where her baby's trouble lay.

She frankly told the physician that she knew why her baby was sick. Her bitter spirit was poisoning the milk in her breast. And the milk was poisoning the child.

She set herself by prayer to overcome that bitter spirit. Her mental attitude was injuring her own body, and her babe's.

The changed mental attitude was followed by a change in her babe's health. The true Christian spirit certainly had a healing effect on both her own body and her child's.

If one's heart is full of a spirit of confidence and love the mother's milk is more nourishing. If one is angry the spittle becomes poisonous; if love dominates the spittle is healing. Love heals one's body. Its reverse hurts the body.

I know intimately the instance of a friend who was under sore stress of spirit regarding one tenderly loved. The thing ran along for a good while.

She was an utterly consecrated Christian. But unconsciously to herself her anxiety was greater than her faith in the outcome. And her hair began to grow gray quite perceptibly.

Some bit of the Book in a time of prayer brought a change. She quit the unconscious worry, and rested, actually rested mentally and in spirit, on the word of Christ regarding the loved one.

And again it was quite noticeable that the graying of her hair stopped. It stopped quite definitely from that time. Those closest to her marked it and spoke of it.

It is a commonplace with the medical fraternity that the mental attitude affects, and affects most seriously, bodily conditions.

It has been demonstrated that anger, fear, and the like, not only check secretions and have a paralyzing effect internally, but actually cause the secretion of poisonous substances within the body.

Faith Runs Fear Out-of-Doors.

Now, the thing to mark most keenly is this: a simple childlike trust in Christ drives that spirit of dread and fear clean out.[1]

It changes radically one's mental attitude. The imagination is radically affected. And that change at once begins to work changes in the body.

It works in three ways. It will actually remove imaginary ills, and also those ills resulting from a tortured imagination. It will actually work toward changing bodily conditions, healing where there has been weakness and disease.

It will tend steadily toward keeping one in prime condition, in full vigour and strength. It will actually ward off disease threatening by contact.

That new mental attitude reacts in a marked way on one's nerves. There is a normal relaxing of tense nerves. Tense nerves are re-

[1] 1 John 4:18.

sponsible for bodily ailments to an incalculable extent. A normal relaxation removes a long list of bodily ills.

The latest expert word on defective eyesight is that it is caused by nervous tension in the eye itself, very largely. It is said that relaxation is the great corrective, making glasses not needed. And this theory is being worked out with some most surprising results.

And, be it marked keenly, all this is simply on the natural level of action. I have tried to make it clear that Christ uses supernatural power in healing when need be.

But this thing I am speaking of now is on the purely natural level. The right touch with Christ affects the mental attitude. And the mental attitude controls largely the functions and sensations of the body.

From a reliable source the incident comes of a famous Philadelphia physician now deceased. The woman who consulted him told the story.

She was of a nervous temperament, and her numerous troubles had worried her to such a degree as to affect her health, and even threatened to affect her mental balance.

The eminent specialist listened, and then quietly told her to read her Bible an hour a day, and report again in a month.

She was indignant. He gently insisted. Reflection led her conscientiously to do as he advised. The change was most marked. On reporting again, she asked the physician how he knew just what she needed.

The famous physician turned to a worn, marked Bible lying open on his table, and said with deep earnestness, "Madam, if I were to omit my daily reading of this Book I would lose my greatest source of strength and skill.

"I never go to an operation, or a distressing case, without reading my Bible. Your case called not for medicine but for a source of peace and strength outside your own mind. I gave you my own prescription. I knew it would cure."

Turning your thought toward Christ fills you with the conception of His reality, His love, His power. Time daily spent over the Book, reaching through to Christ, brooding thoughtfully about Him, all this brings that attitude of heart and mind commonly called *faith*.

It fills your heart with love, love for Him. And love, this drawing of you out tenderly toward Him, this casts that slavish fear out.

You don't try to turn it out. You're thinking of Christ. He draws your heart out to Him. You resist the fear. It goes. The love drives it out. You find it gone.

Now note, that simple faith in Christ does two things. It *releases* that natural creative healing power within your body. That power swings into action. Its power is beyond calculation. At least, nobody has yet calculated it fully or adequately.

It does a second thing. It opens the way for any direct supernatural touch needed in addition to that natural creative healing power. It was in the days of his wisdom that Solomon said, "A tranquil heart is the life of the flesh."[1]

Now this is the first of the two main things we are talking about, the *right mental attitude* which comes as a *natural result* of a simple, true faith in Christ.

This is the first half of the chapter of what happens. But, mark keenly, it is only half. There's a second half.

The Body—Master or Servant?

The second thing that will mark the true Christian is—what? obedience? That is only part of the answer. Shall I say obedience to God's laws?

Again that doesn't tell it out fully. It is this, obedience to Christ *in everything,* and this includes *the common laws of health.*

Now, some saintly folk will begin to think that this is rather dropping to a low level. "The laws of our *body!*" you say.

The truth is it is climbing up a bit for most of us. Oh, yes, I know you say you would gladly sacrifice bodily comforts and strength for Christ's sake. And you mean it.

Yes, but you need to be on your guard lest you are disregarding the law of your body *for your own sake,* because of what you prefer, or don't prefer.

And, *and,* this may deprive Christ of the messenger He needs. You may be giving Him a poorer crippled service when you needn't. And

[1] Proverbs 14:30.

it may be in an emergency when your poorer service, your failure, slows up His plans.

For *Christ's sake*, in the thick of the emergency of life, the true Christian seeks to make his body the strongest possible, the most disciplined channel through which Christ's power may flow. And this is done through a thoughtful obedience to its laws.

This is keeping "the body under," under the control of that Christ passion. Disobeying its law, carelessness, not-thinking, may be letting your body get the upper hand.

It gets from under, up on top, hindering your best service. Christ has been robbed of the needed service of many a saintly child of His, through unconscious thoughtless disregard of his body, or worse.

The touchstone of the Christian life is the same as the touchstone of the true human life, *obedience*. But obedience is not a matter of doing or not doing certain things.

It's on a higher level than that. It's doing as a certain One wants or would prefer. Not "things," but "a Person" holds your eye. It's getting or keeping in better shape for the errand He has sent you on.

The thing that seems small or trivial in itself is now thought seriously about. Because so you can be a truer Christian in your conduct, and so you are better fitted for what that One wants done, and more serviceable to your fellows.

It's astonishing the commonness of indifference to, and disobedience of, the rhythmic laws of health, among not only good but really saintly people.

Such disobedience or indifference or carelessness in other matters would rule a man out of life. It would make him a forced exile.

He couldn't keep a bank account without careful obedience to the laws of the bank. He couldn't run an automobile, nor be a student in any sort of college or school, nor run a successful business, nor move in polite society, nor be member of a club. Obedience to law (a recognized agreed-upon sequence of action) is the commonplace of all intercourse.

And the thing moves up to a wholly higher level when it concerns a Christian, and especially when it concerns his body. For the Christian aims to live the truly ideal life in a practical way, for *Christ's sake,* as well as for his own.

And his body is the fine tool he works with. He'll surely keep his tool in the best possible shape all the time for the sake of the work it does.

The true Christian takes pains to learn about his body, and to think into its need, that so he can be free of his body, free to do his work.

Obedience means intelligence, being informed, becoming skilled. So the habit of a wise obedience is formed, and one is strong and free. One thinks about his body so he can forget it in the thick of his work.

It is striking that the Book of God gives the

principles of everything we need. There are the two models here for the bodily life. The earliest is Adam in Eden before the serpent got in.

The second is the model of God's messenger nation. It is much fuller and more explicit, because the serpent had gotten in. And now there are things to guard against. These have been already spoken of.

Recalling these two models, there are some six things that the thoughtful Christian will think about, so he needn't think about them when absorbed in his work.

In a sane, intelligent way he will think about and form certain habits. Then he is free to do something worth while.

Six or Sick?

These six things are, food, air, exercise, sleep, cleansing, and posture. Just a few words about these.

The body needs *food*. It needs enough. It is hurt by too much. How much? Enough to keep it strong and fit, *and* no more.

It has become quite a commonplace that we all eat too much. Drunkards and topers are supposed to be gone, but eat-ards, and food topers, are still in abundant evidence.

Much of our strength is taken up in digesting food that tasted good, but adds nothing to our strength. Indeed it takes from strength and makes us less fit.

The sense of taste shouldn't decide what we

eat. It has its important place. But, knowledge of food, the sense of taste, and keeping fit for one's work, these together should decide.

The body needs food of the sort that will keep it in the best fighting shape. One naturally believes that the Creator thought about our bodily needs in the provision He made.

For instance, wheat has in it numerous substances that our bodies need. If commercialism takes most of that nourishment out, so the whitened product can be stored without spoiling and loss of money, one naturally avoids such a product.

Using it is robbing his body of certain things it *must* have for health and vigour. And this same sort of thinking can be applied to all foods.

If the way the food is cooked washes much or most of it away, the finer, subtler elements, clearly the body isn't getting something it needs. A man may be partially starved, even with a loaded table, and a full stomach.

Proportion of food figures in. Adam in Eden reached *up* for his food. He had a fruit and nut diet. It was all sun-cooked.

After the Flood Noah reached down as well as up. He added the things that grew under and close to the soil. And he added animal food.

That would suggest that the original diet was a fruit and nut diet. It would suggest that flesh food was only one of three sorts. That puts it in a minor place. This suggests proportion, a balancing of one's food.

But all life has greatly changed. It is not normal. What is absolutely best (outside of morals), is very often not best under certain circumstances. And this change affects our bodies and their need.

If a Christian man, that is a really human man, finds that much less meat and more of the succulent and leafy vegetables and the juicy fruits, day by day, helps him to be less irritable, and in better control of his temper, he will be quick to make the change.

For the life is more than food, much more, his Christian life. And in that case he will find his body stronger too.

The thoughtful man comes to know that a radical change takes place in his body about the time an initial four gets into his age. The building stage is past. It required certain foods that go to building the body up to its maturity.

Now, as he passes that line of bodily change, food is taken simply to repair the waste of his day's work.

More than that much adds excessive weight, which itself is a diseased condition, and leads to other diseased conditions. Weight over normal is a diseased and abnormal condition.

The great insurance companies are modifying their standard tables of age and weight. The standard of weights is being made less. Money sharpens their wits.

The thoughtful man comes to find that after a certain age a smaller quantity, the lessening or omitting of the heavier foods (meats, eggs,

Human Side of Healing

and the like), actually adds to his physical and mental vigour.

And as a Christian he does this, for it affects his Christian character, and his usefulness to his Master.

It is notable that the common diet of many nations runs so largely to the meat-potato-white-bread sort of food, and so little to the succulent and green leafy vegetables and juicy fruits.

Yet the dietary experts insist on the necessity of a balanced diet, and especially a lessening of the heavier foods and an increase of the lighter, in middle life and after.

The thoughtful Christian thinks into these things in a sober, sane, sensible way because he is a Christian. He adjusts his habits. So he keeps his body under control.

And so he is freer and stronger for his life task. And there is a fine, quaint homeliness in the way the Holy Spirit guides in just such things.

I recall an unusually saintly man of New York City, a great Christian leader, much blessed in service, a layman, of full bodily habit.

He had a serious illness. He taught healing, and had experienced it. But now it didn't come. And he wondered why. There's a special bit of holding quiet in spirit, and waiting on God in prayer, to know if there was anything hindering.

And, he said, in my presence, that an answer came. It was in a single word. It was the name of a certain kind of meat of which I imagine he may have been rather fond.

He said that quiet inner voice uttered distinctly one word, "pork." As he told the story he said, pointing to a Bible, "It was *there*, but I hadn't obeyed it." I am not discussing pork just now. The thing is both simpler and deeper. The Holy Spirit teaches regarding the homely things, if we want to know.

Man is *an open air being*. Our abnormal modern life, called (or miscalled) civilization, has made him an indoors animal. One of the most prevalent disease plagues, tuberculosis of the lungs, is an indoors disease.

There is no question that the common indoors habit both weakens and shortens life. As things actually are we can't live a wholly outdoors life.

But the nearer we can come to it the nearer we are to the true full normal human. And no words are adequate to tell the physical blessedness of sleep in the open air. There is nothing that so rebuilds and cushions one's nerves.

All out-of-doors air is good air, night and day. God's air is always good. It's the shut-up, warmed-up, used-over-and-over-again, air that poisons us.

Habitual deep breathing, thorough ventilation of every space used, and particularly all the out-of-doors air it is possible to get, this is native to us. And the more we can actually stay out in the open the nearer we come to normal conditions.

And the body needs *exercise*. Most of us have to work with our bodily strength for a living, and that gives a certain amount of exercise. Though modern life is apt to make it partial and quite onesided.

Watch your baby on the floor twisting and stretching strenuously, pulling and turning. That's its exercise. That helps it digest the food, and keep healthy and grow.

Walking is by far the best single exercise. No one thing is so good for health as an easy swinging walk, with easy shoes, and loose fitting clothing, and head up, and chest out, and arms swinging.

One can walk away any weakness or disease. The exceptions are few. Graduated walking, beginning with little and increasing gradually, until several miles are easily done, will work wonders simply in getting and keeping in bodily vigour. And the mental stimulus and spirit refreshing keep pace.

And so, very soberly, one says that the true Christian walks for health, for *Jesus' sake*. For so he is more usable. He can be of better service to his fellows. And he finds the zest, the sheer zest, of being alive.

If the editor of a religious paper finds that an hour's easy swinging walk to his desk or away from it, clears his brain, and steadies his nerves, and sharpens his sentences, and makes clearer and simpler his pen-preaching and teaching, *if* so, he'll never miss that walk.

He is a better editor, a better religious teacher. Men and women are helped more. Christ has a fuller use of him. He could now write a helpful article on walking as a means of grace.

But exercise should be on the baby system. It should include everything from toes to hair, and out to finger-tips.

Ten minutes given, morning and night, with loose garments, in the open air or at an open window, to a simple series of stretching exercises, regardless of age, is a necessity for vigorous health.

The advertising columns are full of suggestion. There are plenty of books to run through. One can make up his own simple series of movements.

The point to be kept in mind is that the body is stretched, thoroughly stretched from head to foot. Watch the baby. He is a good teacher of how to do it. Or the cat after a nap.

The item of *sleep* gets in without any effort. Some people ought to wake up. But some ought to sleep more. Sometimes sleep is a confession of faith, when it's sleep time and your body needs it, but anxiety keeps you awake, or your nerves.

The thoughtful Christian thinks about his sleep until a good sleep-habit is fixed. These nerve-racking days one must sleep.

And the earlier in the night it is started the better. Sleep before midnight *is* beauty sleep, because it is strength sleep.

One plans for enough, sometimes foregoing something else. He thinks about the details that help sound, deep, refreshing sleep. Sleep renews the strength while food repairs waste.

If the mother finds that a half-hour's lying

down in a quiet room in daytime, whether sleep comes or not, makes her more patient and gentle with the children, and with better self-control in the home, she will prayerfully plan for it.

So she is a truer Christian mother, and shapes better the children's character, present and future. She becomes more serviceable to her Master.

And *cleansing* figures in so much bigger than any of us takes in. It is of two sorts, inner cleansing and outer. There are people who bathe fastidiously who would be shocked at their filthy condition inside.

Health, it is sometimes said, is dependent on three things, food, assimilation, elimination. That is, enough of the right sort of food, the ability to digest and absorb it into the body, *and* the prompt full throwing out of all the waste.

It is surprising how much waste there is to be thrown out. Nature provides two ways for its removal, through the skin and through certain inner organs.

So many diseases are dirt diseases. Often the disease that comes is merely nature trying to get rid of this accumulation of filth.

A healthful body takes care of its own waste products. Careful, prayerful obedience to the laws of the body makes a healthful body.

Careless indifference is pretty apt to make the body very dirty, *inside*. Bathing, and especially preserving the bodily rhythm, are not beneath the attention of the thoughtful Christian.

And *posture* figures in much bigger than one

suspects. We Americans are great sinners in the matter of posture. Man is the one upright animal of all creation. But that fact is slurred over this side the salt water.

Our American habit of slumping down in the chair, sitting on the small of the back, drooping the shoulders and the like, is a serious thing.

The vital organs are crowded for space. The whole inner machinery is badly disturbed. The habit of upright posture, standing and sitting and walking, affects one's health enormously.

But proper posture is impossible without easy-fitting low-heeled shoes. Nothing is more injurious to the whole inner organism than these strange high heels.

The Blood is the Life.

There's a significant sentence in the Book, "the blood is the life." There is much said all through the Scriptures about blood. And there is the deep spiritual significance in much of it referring to the sacrifice of Christ.

But quite apart from that teaching just now, there is here a great truth for our bodily health. The blood is indeed the life of our bodies.

The stomach makes it, the heart pumps it, the lungs purify it, proper exercise keeps it in proper circulation. The whole bodily rhythm is concerned with the blood, its quality and quantity and its being kept moving just as planned.

Good blood, in right quantity, kept moving naturally through the body, means full vigorous life. Poor blood, not enough blood, means a poor defective quality of life. Bad blood means diseased life. Congested blood, too much in one part and too little somewhere else, means disorder, disease.

Enough blood, not too much, of the right quality, not too rich, in normal circulation, gives vigorous abundant physical life. Any slip at any point means either defective or diseased life. And the sort of food decides the sort of blood.

There are two purposes in bathing. The common use, of course, is for cleansing. The other purpose is to help circulation of the blood, and so through that affect the health in a radical way.

An old German priest years ago became famous for his so-called water cure. And water cures sprang up everywhere. The dear old man thought it was simply some virtue in the water. And of course that part is true.

But the thing goes much deeper than that. It is the application of varying temperatures to the body through the medium of water. This affects the disturbed congestion of blood.

Cold water drives the congested blood away. Hot water draws it to where it is needed. The skilful application of various temperatures radically changes the circulation of the blood. And it is astonishing how long a list of bodily ills can be quite removed in this way.

There's a lot of natural healing and of health in our bath tubs if one knew how to use them in this way.

On the same principle walking in the bare feet

on the grass in the dew of the morning acts as a stimulant.

Nature hurries warm blood to the feet to relieve the sense of cold. The excess of blood in the head or somewhere else is relieved.

There is no finer tonic for tired brain or overwrought nerves than walking in bare feet on the cool dewy grass. Care should be taken not to let the feet be cold afterward.

All this sort of talk may seem rather trivial and homely to some good saintly folk. But, *but*, if the tired-out preacher Sunday night finds that dipping his feet in sharply cold water, repeatedly, for a few minutes, and then drying thoroughly, and maybe a bit of friction on the soles,

If, I say, he finds this steadies his nerves and refreshes his brain, plainly he can be of more service to his congregation. Their sleep can be postponed until after the church service is over.

For the shortest road to a nervously tired, aching head is usually through the feet. The two ends may meet helpfully in that case. Proper care of the feet is often the surest way to help the head. And this includes easy natural sort of shoes.

If that same preacher finds that the habitual daily scrubbing of the soles of his feet with a stiff nail-brush full of lather clears the cobwebs out of his weary head,

And so, makes the sermon better, the sentences clearer and sharper, the words simpler, the illustrations bite in better, and the people helped for the morrow's task, he is surely likely to wear that nail-brush out at a lively rate, and then get another.

He's glad to do it *for Jesus' sake,* and for the sake of the crowd, too, that needs help for the daily round.

If a Christian man finds that plunging his head repeatedly into a deep bowl of cold water, doing it cautiously till he gets somewhat used to it, and being sure the hair is bone-dry afterward, *if* he finds that that sends the excess of blood in his head elsewhere, where it is needed, and there's a sense of refreshment, isn't he likely to do it? Just because he's a Christian?

He's an easier man to live with now. He makes a better father and husband, and worker and neighbour. He becomes a better Christian in his daily contacts. Surely anything that will help like that, he'll do, for Christ's sake.

These are the six things suggested by those two old models of personal life, food, air, exercise, sleep, cleansing, and posture. They come under the head of obedience, the second of the two main things we are talking of just now.

Nine Bodily Sins.

Some of the commonest sins are not classed as sins at all. Yet they *are* sins against our bodies, *and* so against Him whose dwelling-place our bodies are.

Here are the nine commonest sins against the body. Too much food and an unbalanced diet, lack of balanced exercise, breathing poisonous indoor air, lack of inner cleanliness, taking poisons into the body in the shape of stimulants, sedatives and drugs, tense nerves, overwork, wrong posture, and the use of the propagating organs otherwise than as intended by nature.

These are responsible for by far the greatest number of diseases. Repentance here would result in most physicians losing their practise. But there seems little need for the physicians to worry on this score.

And obedience, intelligent, thoughtful, sensible obedience, to the requirements of our bodies would quite remove them. The exceptions are decidedly in the minority.

Of course, overwork is one of the commonest sins among conscientious Christians. It may come through a lack of judgment. Most times it is, at root, evidence of a lack of faith in Christ, *practically*.

There are no breakdowns in the path of obedience. But the path of service is strewn thick with saintly wrecks.

The touchstone of the true life is, not the crowds and their need, not service, not suffering nor sacrifice.

The touchstone is obedience, simple, clear, intelligent, full obedience to the Holy Spirit's plain leading. And when in doubt, wait.

There's a Lord to the harvest. There's a Chief-of-staff. The ordering of strategy and tactics and movements is with Him. Our part is the quiet heart, the open ear, the trained discernment for His voice, His leading. And then doing as He leads, *and only that.*

But, *but,* the thing to remember constantly is this. It is Christ's will to forgive the truly penitent, and to heal their bodies.

And He is at your side now eagerly waiting to do whatever is needed.

VII

GOD'S SCHOOL OF SUFFERING: CAN WE HASTEN GRADUATION DAY?

It is Christ's first will that we should be made pure in heart, intelligent in understanding the Father's will, with a passion for doing it, clean out of touch with everything that doesn't help that way, in warm touch with our fellowmen, inflexibly set against every sort of evil, and always strong and healthful in body.

Guard Your Strong Points.

EXPERIENCE is the best teacher, and charges the biggest fee. It insists on being paid, day by day, as you go along. No book accounts allowed, nor credits.

You don't pay in cheap stuff like gold and engraved paper and checks. No, you pay in blood and sweat. You pay in your own life given slowly out, sometimes painfully out, under tense pressure.

But you get something. You get much. You get most. You get the one real thing, gold, real gold, the gold of character; you yourself, your changed self, that's what you get. You're never the same again.

Experience means what you go through, and what goes through you. Our knowledge is really limited to just that. We know only what we go through.

God's School of Suffering

What is woven into the fabric of actual life, that we really know, and only that. The rest we only know *about*. And there's a whole solar system of difference between the two.

Bodily pain bends the most stubborn will. And that is saying a great deal. For there is nothing harder to bend than a stubborn will.

The will is never broken. It can't be. It can only be bent, and that means bent from within. No man's will, however obstinate, can be bended, however slightly, except from within. That is to say, by his own choosing to bend it.

Every man is an absolute sovereign in his will, from his mother's breast until the breast of old mother-earth enfolds him at the last. This is the way God made him.

But bodily pain, cutting, eating in, and then getting sharper-toothed, and persisting, tirelessly persisting, day in and day out, by night and day, awake and asleep, and when you can't sleep, that is the sorest pressure that can be brought to bear on a man's will. It is the whip with the ugliest lash and sting.

This explains much bodily pain, not all, but much. For there is nothing more mulishly stubborn, in earth or heaven or the depths below, than a stubborn human will. Perhaps you know that. And there is nothing so relentlessly persistent as bodily pain can be. It is a fierce conflict, many a time.

Often it is stubborn self-will and Love in fierce competition. The self-will refuses to bend even when it knows it should, that it's right to, and best to. For stubbornness can become a habit gripping a man beyond his own heart's wish.

And Love, with a breaking heart over the pain being suffered by that stubborn will, yet keeps the fire burning more fiercely, *to save the man's life.*

One can be strong enough to be stubborn, but not strong enough to bend. The will is really strongest when it uses its strength in bending to a higher, better, wiser, will.

But Love wins out. The exceptions are rare. The heart, after all, wins in competition with the will. It kindles gentle fierce fires under the will, and keeps them burning, tender and hot, till the will yields, mellows, bends, capitulates.

The one thing greater than a stubborn will is a true, tender, hot heart. Love wins. This is the great lesson in God's School of Suffering.

A man's strong point is apt to become his weak point, when he's out of full touch with God. A man may come to have the possible weakness of his strongest qualities. Away from the steadying touch of God's presence the pendulum swings clear to the opposite limit. Abraham was called a friend of God because he believed Him. His faith in God staggered not at the humanly impossible. Yet he quite failed God, twice, in going to Egypt and so imperilling God's world plan; and in the Hagar incident.

Moses was the meekest man, and no one ever lost his temper so badly and completely. David

God's School of Suffering 155

was one of the saintliest of men, and no man has given more opportunity to men to revile because of that ugliest moral blot in his life.

Solomon was the wisest man, at the beginning. He became the stupidest moral fool, and so continued to the end.

Elijah's boldness and daring made a record, yet he ran away with cowardly swiftness from a woman's threat.

Job was esteemed the most patient of men, but was there ever a greater exhibition of hot, intolerant impatience than in his replies to his critics? He was the humblest of saints, and quite unconsciously showed how proud a man could be.

One should keep a keen eye on his strong points. And the eyesight is keenest here when the knees are bent.

There is simply no telling what may happen to any of us when we lose full touch with Christ. The Spirit of God is man's native air. Away from that he certainly gets into bad shape, and does the queerest unlikeliest things.

Man is free, utterly free, *in* his will. That's God's tenderest touch. In that he is most like God. He becomes a slave, a rank slave, shackled and chained, *to* his will. It's a bit of the ugly trail of sin, the getting out of touch with God.

It's Christ's *first* will that we should be strong and well in body. But what a time of it He has getting His first will done.

Some of the saintliest of people, so lovable and gentle personally, have such stubborn wills. Let us hope it can be said truly that it is quite *unconsciously* that they *won't* yield their will to God's, in some cherished particular.

We all seem to be a bit set in our own way. Some saintly folk are so sure they know better than God, *in certain things*.

One tries hard to believe it is always an unintentional stubbornness. Maybe putting it so baldly will help the truth break in through that same saintly stubbornness.

And so there has to be a term of school. Many a dear saint supplies the scholar and the entrance conditions for the school of suffering.

And the discipline seems stiff and stern. And the fees are very high. And they are payable daily, and collected too. And the lessons seem hard and the time long.

But then Love is always the schoolmaster, real Love, tender and true, honest and courageous, uncompromisingly insistent on the highest ideals.

One hand tenderly and patiently is underneath strengthening and sustaining, while the other guides and steadies, limits and lessens, the discipline when possible. And the Schoolmaster's eye watches the calendar hoping for an early graduation. And His heart watches with deepest concern the scholar, who alone fixes the graduation date.

We learn best by stories and pictures. The story is the picture for the ear. The picture is the story for the eye. We learn most through the eye, with the ear a close second.

There are three stories in this solitary old

Book of God, pictured stories with the warm, vivid colouring of real human life, that come in here.

There's Job at one end, Paul at the other, and Jacob in between. Any one of them is quite enough to tell the story of Love's schooling, all three together pile things up to the irresistible point.

Job the Scholar.

There's an unusual fascination about the Job story. It is told so fully, and made so vivid, and is so human. It is the first of all these books to be written down. It is put at the gateway into this old Book of God.

There is purpose in all this. For it deals with the sorest question of human life through the ages, the problem of suffering. Here, simply told, put into men's hands at once, is God's own answer to the problem. And it proves an answer that answers. It is full and adequate.

It is striking that there are two parts to the story. The first has caught the eye of the Church; the second part has been strangely slighted, indeed ignored.

Yet the story is not complete, and the answer not understood, unless and until both parts are taken together. It is one story.

There are six chapters in the story, all told. In part one there are five chapters. In part two there is just one chapter.

But what a chapter this sixth, this last chapter, is. It fairly vibrates with bubbling-over joy.

Music and exuberant singing fill the air. Laughter and congratulation, praise to God, and happy fellowship among men echo everywhere.

The sun is shining. The birds burst their throats with song. The very air is a-thrill with human gladness. And the music is now in the major key. The minor chording that swept and wept all through part one now becomes a blessed undertone to make the joyousness of the major stand out in bolder relief.

How strange that the last bit of the Job story has been so ignored. The graduation day exercises have been strangely pigeonholed out of sight. Did some one behind the scenes have a hand in that?

Look a bit, briefly, at the six chapters of the Job story. Chapter one is *the scholar in school*. The picture is drawn as men saw him. It tells his common reputation in the whole countryside. He was perfect and upright in all his dealings with his fellows.

There was more, he reverenced God, and earnestly sought to please Him. He was thoughtfully and intelligently deliberate in this.

When there had been a time of feasting and convivial enjoyment in the family he was careful to have a special time of prayer afterward, that if anything had been done or said displeasing or not-pleasing to God it might be forgiven, and so no unsuspected root of wrong-doing be allowed.

It was his conscientious habit to be pleasing

to God in the whole habit of his life. And he was careful to guard the life of his growing family.

All this was commonly known. He was the leading citizen in the community. And this was his reputation. He was upright with others, a thoughtful father in his family, and saintly in his own personal life.

His very name suggests his character. Names grew up in those days, up out of a man's character. Here the name given has a distinctly spirit significance. That would be natural with such a man, for his saintliness, his spiritual habit of character, was the outstanding trait. He was called *Job*, that is, the man hated, hounded, persecuted to the utmost possible limit.

His character made him hated. He was heartily disliked by those of the opposite ilk. Especially he was hated by the unseen spirit prince of evil, whose personality in that early day was never questioned.

This is the picture men saw, a man so conscientious, so upright, so thoughtfully methodically righteous and saintly as to arouse opposition in some quarters.

There's another bit in the picture of the man that comes out later in the whole story. It was the side that God saw, the *in*side of his character.

He was so humble that, probably quite unconsciously, he was proud of it. There was a subtle unsuspected inner satisfaction with his spiritual attainments.

What a strange bit of irony, pride in being humble! But a snake may crawl noiselessly through the greenest grass, and among the most fragrant flowers.

He was so conscientious in planning the whole habit of his life as pleasing to God that he slipped a bit in the real thing.

Without being aware of it that very conscientiousness, and methodical care, and saintliness of habit, got in to his inner subconsciousness even more than God Himself.

He would have been the first to pull himself up had he recognized the tendency. He was quick as a flash on his face when God actually spoke to him, and things got straightened out.

But that's the man, the scholar in the school, the two men in one, the man his neighbours saw, and the man God saw.

That's chapter one.[1] Men saw a humble godly man. God saw a bit of dross in the rare fine gold of this man's character.

Job—First Session of School.

Chapter two is the *first session of school*. In the upper spirit realm there's a reviewing of things down on the earth.

Satan is spoken of for the first time in the Scriptures, and spoken of by that name, the Satan, the accuser, the hater, the hounder of men.

God takes the initiative regarding Job. This

[1] Job 1: 1–5.

is significant. There's a purpose at work. God speaks of the well-known character of Job.

Satan maliciously slanders Job as an utterly selfish man who finds it to his advantage to be righteous. Satan is given permission to interfere in Job's affairs, but within strict limitation.[1]

Then the scene of the story shifts to the earth again. Job's opportunity has come. The door up-stairs is to open at his feet.

War, marauding bands, lightning, a terrific wind-storm, these come one after the other with a rush. And everything is swept away, children and possessions one after another in quick succession.

And there is a terribly dramatic piling up of the calamities as the story is told, by one breathless messenger after another, to Job.

And in this sore hour of bereavement, with torn and bleeding heart, Job never flinched in his simple trust in God, and his unfailing personal devotion to Him. Things have gone awfully bad. But there's no reproach in Job's heart.

It is significant that the immediate origin of his trouble is quite unrecognized. He supposes that it is God Himself in action doing all this.[2] It gives emphasis to his humble, uncomplaining submission to God, though he can't understand *why* such things should happen to him.

Again the scene shifts to the upper realm, and

[1] Job 1:6–12.
[2] Job 1:21.

162 About the Healing Christ

again God speaks of the righteousness of Job, though so sorely tried. And again Satan slanders and imputes selfish motives. And now the restriction on Job's person is withdrawn, within a strict limit.[1]

Then comes the touch on Job's person. One of the worst plagues known in that sub-tropical climate, ulcerous sores, known as the black leprosy of Egypt, this breaks out in Job's body. God's gracious protecting restraint is partially withdrawn, for a brief time.[2]

And poor saintly Job, sitting on an ash heap, scraping his itching sores with the sharp edge of a broken piece of crockery, quite takes hold of one's heart.

Then his wife loses heart, and incoherently, bitterly cries out against God. And that doesn't make things any better certainly. It's a bitter draft to swallow when a man doesn't feel his wife by his side, close up, steadying and believing in him.

His wife's unfailing touch and presence and atmosphere strengthens a man quite beyond words. Its absence is felt keenly now, even though the answering voice is still quiet and steady.

Then the three neighbours come. They are supposed to be comforters, deeply grieved over their old neighbour's sore plight. For seven silent days and seven yet more silent nights they sit looking.

[1] Job 2: 1-6.   [2] Job 2: 7-13.

Peering aslant and direct, at Job and at each other, with never a word spoken, but many a thought thought, they sit.

That was the decisive stroke. Job broke under that. His keen ear heard their unspoken thoughts. His sensitive spirit felt the cutting edge of those peering eyes.

Loss of property, loss of children, loss of health, loss of his wife's sympathetic fellowship, he stood up under these.

But, loss of his sacred privacy, and then the criticism all the keener and more cutting because unspoken, and all this continued unbroken seven full days and seven sleepless nights, that was a terrific climax. Job broke under that. Little wonder!

The time test is the hardest test. The patience of patient Job ran out. He was a cunning strategist that planned that campaign, devilishly, cruelly, heartlessly cunning. This is chapter two, the first session in school.

Job—Inside.

Then comes chapter three, *the unsuspected man inside is revealed.*[1] "After this," this sevenfold cunningly piled-up climax of attack, Job "cursed his day."

That is, tacitly, quite unintentionally in all probability, he cursed God who gave the creative touch that day of birth.

And for bitterness of spirit, biting sarcasm, persistent absorption in his own integrity and in

[1] Job 3: 1–31: 40.

the unfairness of all that's happening to him, for rebellion against God and God's dealings, it would be difficult to match Job in the flood of talk that is now loosened out.

How pain itself, with no touch of grace allowed in, sharpens the tongue, makes picturesque rhetoric, and puts acid in the spittle! It's immensely suggestive.

The three critics, called comforters, go at him in turn. And the burden of their talk is this: all these calamities mean that God is acting in judgment on Job for his wickedness.

They insist that all his godliness is a mere sham to cover up the utter selfishness and actual wickedness underneath. Their talk hangs well together. There's thorough consistency.

It is full of pious phraseology, inaccuracies, half truths, and positive untruths. It's a queer tangle and mixture. It has a strangely familiar modern sound.

It is not difficult to understand who sent them, or which side they represent in this pathetic conflict going on, on the battlefield of Job's life.

It's the last stroke of that carefully planned attack. One should be careful with quotations from the Book of Job, to note whose words are being quoted.

But Job out-talks them. As the debate goes on their talks get shorter, his longer. He talks nine times, all three of them eight times. He says half as much more as they.

His bitterness increases. At last they quit. They are talked out. The case is hopeless to

God's School of Suffering 165

them because this man Job is so set in believing in his own righteousness. They give Job up as a hopeless incorrigible.

This is the first session of the school. The examinations show Job up in rather bad shape. Job lays himself bare. He is indeed a rare saint in the utter integrity of his heart and life.

But he doesn't understand. He is in the dark. And he blunders badly. That's why the story is put down here, so his spirit kinsfolk need not make the same blunders.

Job questioned God's love, which is always above question or suspicion. Because he doesn't understand he questions God's love, which means he doubts it.

And in the sore experience, certain unsuspected things that were inside came out. They must have been in or they couldn't have come out. As you see them coming out you know that, all unsuspected, they were hidden away inside.

It's a strange sight indeed this. Saintly Job, rarest of saints in the purpose of his heart, and the uprightness of his conduct, unconsciously letting the seamy side stick out,

Sitting on the ash heap, talking, with the sharp-edged bit of broken crockery in rhythmic motion on his itching scabs, declaring his own righteousness, and reviling God and God's dealings. Cutting sarcastic flings intermingle with insistence on his faith in God.

The examinations go hard with Job. They show up something inside never suspected. He doesn't see it yet. Job's weakness is laid bare. His humility is the last thing in view now. Indeed it's clear out of view, lost sight of.

And where *is* the proverbial patience of patient Job? All this rebelliousness of spirit against God, this biting, burning sarcasm, this utter absence of the love spirit, this utter depressed absorption in himself, this exaggerated ego, this had all been in, quite unsuspected. Else it couldn't have gotten out.

One begins to understand now about that school of suffering. The graduate, with honours, of many schools is having a final post-graduate course. God wants him up higher, highest, with full honours, but forgetting all about the honours in thinking about his wondrous God.

Now comes chapter four, *God's teacher comes*.[1] The second session of school opens. God takes a hand in things indirectly. He sends a messenger, Elihu. Elihu is a *teacher*. And what poor saintly righteous Job needed above all things just now was a teacher.

His heart was all right, but his understanding of things was muddled. The teacher quietly, patiently, gently, plainly, teaches. Then Job's eyes begin to open. New soft light begins to break in.

First of all this teacher explains just *why* all this has happened to Job. He repudiates utterly what the three critics had been declaring so positively.

God had *not* been acting in judgment on Job.

[1] Job 32:1–37:24.

The whole thing is on a wholly higher level, a love level, a wooing level.

Elihu points out that Job had been insisting on his own integrity. He was rebelling bitterly because of what had happened to him, and against God's dealings with him, and so against God Himself.[1]

Job had been proud of his sanctity, the utter uprightness of his conduct, and the sincerity of his heart. He had become absorbed with himself, his saintliness. He was proud of being so humble, quite unconsciously.[2]

For pride is simply being taken up with yourself in any degree or any way, and not getting God in in His own place.

Humility is simply letting God in to one's thought and imagination and purpose *as big as He really is*. All we have is from God, a direct gift to be held in trust.

Talents, gifts, powers, possessions, everything is given by Him. It is a trust in the full legal meaning of that word, and then the higher love meaning.

All these gifts are at their best only as God's touch is upon them in full, which means, is upon *you* in full.

No one is true to himself, and to his powers, and to his neighbours, except as all is yielded up to God's touch, full constant touch.

And when that's so the mind, the imagination, the will, are all absorbed with the thought of

[1] Job 33: 8–12.
[2] Job 33: 17.

God Himself, His love so beyond words, and all that grows out of His love.

Pride is the assertion of one's self. Humility is being so taken up with some One else that one thinks of himself only in relation to that One.

Then in a simple, practical, wholesome way all one's powers, one's relation to his fellows and to the day's task, fall into right place. That's the touch upon you of this One you're so taken up with.

That absorption in God, in Christ, is a very practical thing. You have seen a babe watching intently the mother's face, utterly absorbed, conscious of nothing else. And the sight has caught your heart.

And so the mother with her babe, a lover with his lover, a husband with a wife. This thing of being absorbed in some one else is common enough to know about, blessedly so.

Job was being wooed from absorption in himself up to the higher level, forgetting himself in seeing God. If ever a man really sees God he loses himself at once. And yet he really gets hold of his true self in losing himself in God.

Elihu gently but firmly puts his finger on the sore spot. Job had been taken up with himself. His whole trouble at root was pride, thinking about himself.[1] That's the teacher's first point, tactfully, clearly made.

Then the teacher goes on. Something happens. Sickness comes. Elihu touches only one

[1] Job 33: 13-18.

God's School of Suffering 169

thing in Job's troubles. But that is enough, and makes things simpler to Job's understanding.

Elihu doesn't go into the matter of the process by which the disease came to Job, just now, as is told in the beginning of Job's story. There's a vivid description of a desperately sick man.[1] That's the teacher's second bit.

Then comes a teacher to make things clear to this sick man.[2] Elihu modestly speaks of himself only indirectly. A paraphrase helps make the thought clearer, a translation into simple English of the underneath thought.

Elihu says, "If there be with the sick man a messenger, a teacher, one in the close, confidential touch of personal love, to explain things to him patiently and gently and clearly;—"

Then comes prayer, and the healing.[3] Now the healed man frankly says, "I have sinned." There's a vast difference between being told you are a sinner and actually confessing yourself that you are a sinner.

Now, healed, the man goes about singing. He is so absorbed with such a wondrous God as he has found all anew that he goes about telling his neighbours and friends about Him.

This is the heart of Elihu's teaching. There are six links in its chain, pride, disease, a teacher, prayer, healing, telling others about this wondrous God.

[1] Job 33: 19–22.
[2] Job 33: 23.
[3] Job 33: 24–28.

And the rest of Elihu's talk, by far the greater part, is taken up chiefly in *talking about God.* Unconsciously he becomes a fine illustration of what he is talking about.

I can imagine that already a bit of restful sigh escapes Job's lips. His thought is sharply changed. What fine psychology! He turns away from himself (what a relief!) to—*God.*[1] That's the close of the second session of school.

Job Sees God.

Then the third session opens. This is the fifth chapter of the story, *Job gets a sight of God.*[2] God speaks. Job hears, and gets down on his face at once. God picks up the thread where Elihu had dropped it, and goes on weaving the same fabric.

And what God does is this, simply this, but all of this: He looks into Job's face. Job never forgot the sight. God talks in a very simple, homely way about Himself.

Job gets a picture of God, the Creator, His intelligence that could think things out, His wisdom that could so skilfully adapt means to end, His power that could actually do what He did; and then above all, running through all and between the lines is this: His love; He did it, actually did what He did.

Job got a picture of God. He never got over it. He's down on his face in the dust. It's a

[1] Job chapters 34–37.
[2] Job chapters 38–41.

remarkable face-about. "Mine eye seeth *Thee*: I abhor *myself*."[1]

And then God graciously gives Job a rare opportunity. It is not a test to see if Job can stand it. It is Job's opportunity to reveal the wholly new spirit now in control. It is his opportunity to be like God.

He is to pray for these poor befogged critics. They certainly need it. And he gladly does it. He is so taken up now with God that everything is affected. The absorbing thought of such a God comes swamping in. It takes possession. It graciously grips him.

The bitter sarcasm toward these critics goes clean out. Love, that is to say, God, fills his heart. He is grateful for the outlet of this new passion. He gladly prays for these men that they, too, may see this wondrous God.

The real God-touch means a humaner human-touch. Job is really humble now, but he doesn't know it. He's so absorbed with God that he quickly forgives and loves his bitter critics. Because that's being like God. That's the God-touch.

When a man thinks he is humble he may know at once that he isn't. He's thinking about himself. When one thinks in his heart that he really *is* saintly, he may know for a truth that he isn't. He hasn't the real thing; for he's taken up with himself.

The real thing of humility is being absorbed with God. Then you become unconsciously like

[1] Job 42: 1-9.

Him. It becomes a passion, an intensely practical passion, to get others in touch, too. That's the God-touch.

Humility is such a sensitive plant, when you think you have it it withers up at once, and dies. This is the third session of school. Job sees God, and gets down on his face, and then reaches out to help others.

Then comes chapter six, *Graduation Day*.[1] School's out. Satan is heard of no more. He has slunk away. Resisted, he fled. The healing touch comes without being asked for. And it's a full healing. It includes body and family and circumstances and length of life.

And the striking thing that catches you at once is this: *Job fixed the date for graduation day*. The whole decision rested with him. His will had new strength now. It could bend, bend to the higher will.

And it did. That was the turning point. That fixed the date. All God's power and love wait on man's consent. We control the door through which God enters our lives.

How long did this school of suffering last? There were three sessions, then graduation day. But how much time did the whole take?

I don't know in actual days and weeks. It doesn't tell. But the story as told gives the impression that the whole thing could have occurred within a few weeks, from new moon to full.

How long did this school last? I do know. I

[1] Job 42:10-17.

God's School of Suffering

know exactly. Just as long as it took Job to get down on his face; then graduation day.

Job could have made it last much longer. Any one can. Some are strong enough to talk humbly about themselves, and submissively. But they're not strong enough to bend, bend clear down.

You've got to get clear down to see God's face, and hear His voice. The best view of God is gotten on your face in the dust. Then the eyes of the spirit open.

And even the ash heap, and that broken piece of crockery, become fragrant memories. For they became the gateway into that blessed change of spirit. And through that the healing and all the rest came.

School fees were never so high. Ask Job. And payment of fees was never more cheerfully assented to, *afterward*, when school was out.

One is quick to note that there is a twofold purpose in this old Job school-story. There was a purpose *for* Job himself.

And there was a purpose *through* Job. Job has been a silent eloquent preacher to men ever since his story was lived in the plains and hills of Uz.

There was a distinct purpose of service in Job's experience. The whole Church, and some day the whole race, will be grateful to Job for being a good scholar in God's school.

Paul's Thorn—The Man.

The second of these outstanding picture-stories is that of Paul, Paul's thorn. Whenever one talks rather positively about prayer, or about bodily healing, some one always remembers and asks about Paul's thorn. Well, there certainly is distinct help for us all here.

First a look at the man, then a look at his thorn. The best light on this troublesome thorn is the man. He, his character, and the great bit of work for God he was chosen to do, these throw the best light on that stinging, sticking thorn.

Paul is a great man from any point of view, and a great saint. His Hebrew blood, his aristocratic family and breeding, his inherited and acquired culture,

His university training, his breadth of outlook, his inflexible conscientiousness, his passion of devotion to his Master, what a man he was among men! What a saint among saints!

What a giant he was in his will. The unflinching unfaltering insistence on his task, in spite of opposition and difficulties, all those arduous journeys in the thick of hardships of every imaginable sort up to the limit of endurance, these all tell what a giant he was in his will.

But, speak softly, his strong will sometimes held the lines too tight. A man's weak point is pretty apt to be the swing-away of the pendulum on his strong point. Paul had the possible weakness of his strongest qualities. He was a bit set in his way.

Say it very softly, for we are talking about dear old saintly Saint Paul. Say it yet more

God's School of Suffering 175

softly, for where one speaks of one weak spot in him he quickly calls to mind a half-dozen in himself. Yet say it distinctly, *to help.*

God had a hard time getting Paul to go *His* way. God found it difficult sometimes to get Paul to fit into *His* plans. Paul had a plan or two of his own. Perhaps just one or two of us may have heard of such a thing before.

From the time of that never-to-be-forgotten experience on the Damascus road, with the light, and the voice, and the overwhelming sense of power, Paul knew that his errand was to the outer non-Jewish world.

The nations of the earth, the Gentiles, this was to be his field of service. The very magnitude of it must have appealed to the imagination of this giant and saint.

But, from the first, he had an intense desire to go to the Jerusalem Jews. He felt he could get them.

It was a perfectly natural thing, for Paul had been so closely associated with them. And his very sense of strategy in action suggested and emphasized it.

He felt in his bones, "I know them. I trained with that group. I know how to take them. Let me at them. If once we can get *them* it will mean so much.

"It's the strategic thing. They crucified Jesus. They stoned the Holy Spirit, in effect, in stoning Stephen. But, *but,* let me at them." This was deep down in his spirit.

Indeed the thing went rather far. Early in

176 About the Healing Christ

his Christian life Christ had given Paul a special vision about this very matter when Paul was praying in the sacred precincts of the temple in Jerusalem.[1]

And the Lord gave him specific directions to get out of Jerusalem, out to the outer non-Jewish world. The Jerusalem leaders were incorrigibly set in their stubborn rejection, he was told.

Then a strange thing happened, passing strange. Paul actually begins to argue with the Lord why he was specially qualified for a Jewish mission!

This was surely taking things to great length, the soldier under orders arguing with the chief-of-staff why he should not do as he was bid, but something else he preferred! Did dear saintly Paul's intensity blur his thinking?

Yet it seems to me, yes, I can recall something of that sort in modern times, and among saintly folk, too. And the temple interview closes with a clear positive command—"Depart; for I will send thee *far hence* (from Jerusalem) to the outer non-Jewish peoples."

And Paul went. With all his splendid powers and devotion he went. But he never lost that early inner passionate longing. He insisted upon it, years after, against distinct intimations of the Holy Spirit in line with that temple interview.[2]

His insistence changed the whole latter part of his outstanding career. That's a little look-in

[1] Acts 22: 17–21.
[2] Acts 21: 4, with references.

God's School of Suffering 177

at this rare saintly giant of God. It explains the thorn that came, and was not taken away.

Paul's Thorn—Healing While Not Healed.

Now, about the thorn.[1] There came some serious ailment in his body. No one knows what it was. The long learned discussions are so much waste breath, when time is so precious and real things so pressing, too.

It doesn't matter a grot what it was. It was there, and it stayed. It interfered. It hurt keenly.

Paul didn't think so much of it, at first. There was Christ to go to. He would go and ask for healing. And the healing touch would come, he felt quite sure.

All Paul's experience would lead him to expect the healing touch. He had that remarkable two years' campaign in Ephesus, where healings to a quite unusual degree were the outstanding feature.[2]

Earlier there had been the man crippled from birth, never able to walk, now leaping and walking through Christ's touch, at the word of Paul.[3]

There is the yet more remarkable bit, toward the latter part, of the young man at Troas on the Ægean, actually brought back from the dead.

And Paul had taught healing. It was part of his group of teachings to the churches wherever

[1] 2 Corinthians 12:7–10.
[2] Acts 19:10–12.
[3] Acts 14:8–10.

he went. He himself had known the healing touch.

He had the best of reason for expecting healing now. Indeed he seems not to have doubted that the healing touch would come. But it didn't.

Again he prays specifically for healing. Still there is no change. The thorn stayed. Its needle-point gets sharper, and sticks persistently in. Ugh! how it hurt! A third time Paul goes to his knees, how earnestly and intensely some of us can understand.

Now, please notice keenly, there's an answer to his prayers. There are three items in the answer. First of all, the man is answered though the petition is denied. Paul is not ignored. His prayer is heard. Christ never ignores any one, nor fails to hear any honest prayer.

The second thing to note is just what Christ said in His answer. I can see dear saintly old Paul one night all alone with his thorn. The day's work is done, the stitching of tent-canvas, and talking to the crowds, and to the two's and three's.

He is tired. He has gone to bed. He would sleep but for that thorn. He turns and twists, and longs for the sleep that doesn't come. And he wonders why the healing touch hasn't come. He is just a bit perplexed, maybe a bit depressed.

Then, quietly, very quietly, a voice comes, an inner voice, quiet as Hermon's dew, clear as the tone of a bell.

God's School of Suffering 179

And the voice said, " Paul, I know about that thorn, and how it hurts. It hurts me, too. It hurts me because it hurts you.

"But, Paul," the voice goes quietly steadily on, " it's a bit better to let the thorn stay, because, only so can I have the use of you, the full free use of you, in *My* plans for the world I gave My life's blood for."

And a hush comes over the dear man's spirit. There comes with the voice a look within. Instinctively Paul begins to understand better. A soft clear light breaks.

He knows, at once, yet better, how true is the word being so gently spoken. He knows that the diagnosis is accurate. And he lies quiet, with a great deep hush in his inner spirit. That's the second bit of the answer.

Then the voice comes again. When the pause has deepened the impression, more comes. The voice goes on in yet quieter gentler lingering tones,

" Paul, I'll be so near you, you will have such a sense of My presence, that you'll forget the thorn even while you feel it cutting in."

Years after I can see the blessed old service-scarred saint in his own hired house in Rome. It's rather late at night.

The crowds have been thronging the house, crowds from all over the world, in this great world centre, Rome. An Egyptian had sat over there, and a dark-skinned Ethiopian yonder.

A cultured-faced man from the Euphrates, and a fair-skinned Caucasian had been standing in the corner side by side. Keen-eyed Greeks, vigorous Latins, alert courtly Spaniards, the cultured and the scholarly, the unlettered and the simple folks, gently jostled each other.

They had crowded in, listening so intently, and questioning so eagerly. And the unseen Presence had been so real. And Paul's heart was all aglow as with a pressure of the hand they had slipped out into the night. Now, they have all gone. Once again the burning Christ message has gone out to the whole world.

Paul is sitting quietly, slowing down inside before seeking bed and sleep. One arm is around young Timothy, not quite so young now. The other hand is laid caressingly upon dear faithful Doctor Luke's arm.

They're talking in subdued tones. And as you listen in you hear Paul say, "Do you know, dear old friends, I wouldn't have missed the thorn for the presence ——"

And the sentence breaks off. A bit of hoarseness, the hoarseness of deep emotion, thickens his voice. And the look of deep reverence and love mingled deepens in his companions' faces.

Then he goes quietly on, "—the presence, the wondrous glory-presence of Jesus, beyond words, that has been with me through it all."

And the clearer light breaks on his listeners. The inner understanding deepens. A great silence falls on them. They know they're at the deep springs.

They are being allowed to see a bit into the Lord's passion for His world, and the place this grayed veteran is having in it. The emergency of sin has gripped both, the unseen One and this man so great in his suffering and in his service.

Yet, yet, there's a bit to add. I am clear, and I grow yet clearer, that our Lord Jesus still prefers to take the thorn away. And He will *if* He may have His way, His *first* way.

Graduation day comes later to Paul. It came one day just outside that city, with an escort of imperial Roman soldiers. Yet, very softly, and still very distinctly, let the words be spoken, it might have come sooner.

But in the mix-up of a strong human will, not unlike other wills we know, and a world in the sore emergency of sin's havoc, and the great passion of the Heart that broke once, things were as they were.

There's something yet farther to note here of much significance. Without any question Paul was repeatedly conscious, indeed continuously conscious of Christ's healing touch on his body through all this rare difficult experience.

As one reads the whole story through the fact is plainly borne in that Christ's healing touch, in protection, in strengthening, and in actual healing, was with Paul through all those thorn years.

It is difficult, if not impossible, to fit in chronologically the beginning of this distressing ailment. But one remembers that Paul had been left for dead just outside Lystra in Asia Minor. And the intense hatred of those Antioch Jews would make them do a thorough job of stoning. Their efficiency is beyond question.

Yet Paul gets up, rests over night, and pushes on the next day. He carried out the itinerary as planned, apparently. That would be an outstanding instance of healing under most extreme circumstances.

And no one can read Paul's own long remarkable list of the experiences he went through without a deep impression of Christ's direct touch on his body throughout.

Listen, and think into, not merely the bodily suffering involved, but the tremendous natural breakdown of bodily strength. Five times he had been whipped on his bare back with forty-stripes-save-one,

And three times with the yet more severe Roman rods save none, once stoned, three times shipwrecked, a night and a day drifting exposed out in the open sea,

The acute hardship of the crude, typical traveling of that time and of the Orient, perils of swollen rivers, of robbers not hesitating to use violence, of hunger and thirst, cold and insufficient clothing.

Think slowly into that list. Clearly enough the experience with the thorn was the more striking to Paul because in the midst of Christ's constant healing touch upon Paul's body.

Paul experienced the threefold healing, the continual protecting restraint upon disease, the strengthening of bodily functions, and the direct positive healing. Else he could never have gone through what he did. The thorn was the more marked as an exception in the midst of such experiences.

The thing that stands out biggest in the whole story here is this: it was for service' sake that this thorn experience was allowed.

It was for the sake of a race of men, swamped by the terrific emergency of sin, and in the scarcity of men at hand available, that the thing occurred.

It was distinctly exceptional. Had it been merely Paul *personally* that was concerned the whole trend of Christ's dealing makes clear that this ailment would have gone like the others. But service controlled. The world's emergency gripped.

Jacob's Limp.

There's one more of these pictures in this rare old gallery of honest portraits, the picture of Jacob at Jabbok.[1]

In that strange night struggle between the sturdy Hebrew herdsman and an unrecognized Assailant, Jacob fully holds his own. Then toward dawn the strange Assailant does a strange thing.

Jacob is startled to feel a slight touch on the inner side of his thigh, and at once the thigh bone goes out of joint.

Instantly Jacob knows that this is no mere man. No man could have done that. And two things at least crowd in faster than he can think.

[1] Genesis 32: 24-32.

His power as a wrestler is clean gone, at once. His native shrewdness makes him think of that. But, far deeper, comes the recognition of who this unrecognized Stranger of the dark is.

He's been fighting against God! And then, all these years he had been fighting against God! and against God's plans for his life! Unconsciously fighting? Half consciously fighting?

At least this much can be said for Jacob, *not recognizing* how much it meant that he had been insistently stubbornly fighting against God, and God's plan. (But then, is that so unusual? and among good people?)

It's the one instance in Scripture of God's own direct touch on a man's body, injuring, laming him. And mark keenly that it was not a disease.

It was a slowing down of the man's gait. He had been so sure of himself. Now he must go through life halting, limping.

Well, there's a purpose under this exceptional act of God's. There's always a purpose where He is concerned. And it is always a purpose of love.

This man Jacob was hindering, actually holding back, and threatening to block completely, God's world plan. It wasn't merely Jacob's own life that was concerned. God's plan for the race hinges on this man.

A man may hinder or break God's plan for his own life, if he will. All God's plans wait on our consent. The sovereign God waits on the sovereignty of man's choice.

But no man can break God's broad plan for the world. He may slow it up. He does that so much. God's sovereignty simply means that, ultimately, through the intricate network of human wills, His great plan will work out, and always in some way *through* man's choice, freely given.

Even now, Jacob could have balked still further. It wasn't merely the touch of *power* on his thigh that won. It was that, plus something more, far deeper and tenderer, the touch of *love* upon his heart.

Jacob could have fought against the power. But the love, the patient waiting, and putting up with his wayward conduct, all these long years, the gracious wooing, in so many ways ——!

He could see it all now. It was this that bent his will at last, from within, to this strong, waiting, loving will of his great God.

Note keenly, that this is *a crisis*. Most reverently it can be said it was *God's* crisis. God's plan was in danger. A world's salvation hung in the balance, hung on this one man's consent to be used, in God's way, in God's plan.

It is a threefold crisis. It was *a crisis of available material*. Jacob was the son of Isaac, the grandson of Abraham, through whom the world plan must be worked out.

He was the twin son, it is true. But the other, Esau, was plainly disqualified by temperament. Impulsive, hot-headed, wholly unreliable, bartering his most sacred possession for something to eat, as unstable as water, he was wholly unfitted for leadership in carrying forward God's plan. God was narrowed down to Jacob.

Jacob was a cool, steady, calculating man of method and habit. He was a thinker and a hard worker. He was a man to do things. But he had the mean moral strain in him. He was intensely selfish. He was forever grasping, cunningly taking advantage of the other fellow. He was unscrupulous. He never hesitated at the most underhanded move to gain his point. Jacob was morally contemptible.

But his failings were moral. Esau's were mental. The moral could be changed by grace, if once Jacob's consent could be gotten.

It was not really that Jacob was the better man, he was the less-poor of the two. It was a crisis of available material. God needs the best. Jacob must be used, but first he must be changed. So the exceptional thing was done.

It was *a crisis of time.* Long years Abraham and Sarah had been wooed, graciously wooed, patiently put up with. Isaac was the child of the changed Abraham and Sarah. He took on their later traits.

And now, for many long years, a full quarter of a century at least, God had been calling Jacob up to the higher level. But Jacob's firmness and strength teetered over into stubbornness. He gets more set.

And he grows more stubborn, more uglily obstinate, more set than ever. Time pressed. It grew less. The stubbornness grew more, and then yet more. In a crisis of time God did the exceptional thing.

It was *a world crisis.* God's plan concerned a world. A Babel, a Flood, a Sodom-and-Gomorrah, tremendous moral catastrophes, these told plainly the moral outcome threatening.

Through Jacob and Jacob's line was to come the little messenger-nation, the Saviour-nation, the Saviour Himself. All unknown, unsuspected by any but God, it was the world crisis. For the sake of the race, to save His great plan for saving a world, God did the exceptional thing.

And, so, by the fords of the Jabbok, under that gentle touch of supernatural power, at the break of a new day, Jacob surrendered his proud stubborn will.

The touch on Jacob's thigh was meant for his heart, like the later touch on the disciples' feet. Jacob felt it there. His heart broke. He had actually been fighting God! He never really meant that.

That heart-breaking touch on the thigh reached into the will, the citadel. The will bent. With all its disciplined strength it bent, and bent clean over.

He quit wrestling. He had to. The disabled thigh settled the wrestling. He took to clinging. And he became the prince, the Israel, prince with God, pleading for forgiveness and blessing, and prevailing.

And God yielded to that penitent clinging plea. God had saved two, the man and the world-plan. So only could it be. The world-plan was saved through the man. No one ever knows how much hangs on his saying "yes" to God.

Jacob learned to walk with God, by *limping*. God tried to get him to walk without the limp. He preferred that. He still does.

Jacob got along faster now because he's been slowed down. He never walked so fast in his life in the true path as now when he goes slowly limping, limping along in his body.

One can well understand that God did what He did reluctantly. It was an emergency transaction. And all the world is in an emergency *just now*. And God is still needing men.

These are the three pictures in this old gallery, Job's ulcerous boils and the ash heap schoolhouse, Paul's needle-pointed thorn, and Jacob's halting limp.

These are three scholars in God's school of suffering. Job graduated early. He learned quickly. It was an intense session but a short one, intensive school work.

Paul's graduation came later, as did Jacob's. Have they had a reunion up there, these three, in the Teacher's own presence, and praised Him out of full hearts? I think likely. But I am quite sure it pleases the Teacher most when we work for early graduation.

One notes keenly that in each case the man concerned was a leader. That makes a great difference. The Devil lays special siege to the leaders. Leaders need more schooling because they touch the lives of so many.

Yet no one lives to himself. None of us can tell what plan of service of Christ's may centre in our glad consent to His personal plan for the life.

In each case it was a crisis, the meeting place of dismal failure and glorious victory. And the man was always the decisive factor.

One recognizes crises best *backwards*. We are so much wiser, *afterwards*. If only we might be quick and true to obey, for Christ's sake, *before* we know it may be a crisis for some one or some plan.

For service' sake, in a crisis, the leader may find things happening. Because so much is hinging, of which he is unaware. If, ah! yes, *if*, one might only obey gladly and fully and quickly, what Christ asks, because He asks, regardless of all else.

Keep Your Hand Out.

And so there may be a waiting time. Bodily healing may be needed, desperately needed perhaps. And we may be in real touch of heart with Christ. And we may pray for the healing touch. And yet, it may not come. There may be a waiting time.

If so, it means simply this: we're needing some schooling. There's some plan involved. And the thing is to be good scholars. Cultivate the keen inner ear and the quiet inner spirit, so we can hear the Teacher's voice. For He is speaking. If we are still enough we'll hear.

But no one expects to stay in school all his

days. We should look forward to a glad graduation day. We should plan early graduation. Our hands should be stretched out, stretched expectantly out, till they grasp what has been promised.

I can never forget my mother's very brief paraphrase of that long verse in the Third of Malachi.[1] The verse begins, you remember, "bring ye the whole tithe *in*," and it ends up with "I will pour" the blessing *out* till you'll be embarrassed for space.

My mother's brief paraphrase was this: *Give all He asks; take all He promises.*

There is always an instinctive hesitancy to speak of one's own personal experiences. They seem so sacred. The reluctance comes unbidden.

And yet, of course, nothing is so strong and convincing, if rightly understood, as actual personal experience. And one is willing to overcome that natural reluctance if only some one may be helped a bit.

Within recent years I went through a critical illness, happily not very prolonged. There was clearly a purpose in it. That has been made quite clear to my inner spirit.

And that purpose was served. That is clear. And one remarkable thing was the distinct touch on the body all during that illness, and in convalescence, overruling the natural course of things.

I have experienced healing in serious matters

[1] Malachi 3:10.

through the use of means prayerfully used. Again, quite distinctly, without the use of means, Christ's own healing touch has come when things were serious.

And yet again, I have been quite clear that it has been Christ's own healing touch, in most difficult circumstances, overcoming the means used, that brought the healing and health.

And, I may add, that while I never have enjoyed better health and vigour than at present, and of late, I am being plainly led in my inner spirit to expect a healing touch beyond what has yet been experienced.

I am still in school, God's school. I have gotten through some of the rooms, but not all. My hand is stretched out day and night. And I have the sweet assurance that graduation day is coming very soon now.

I heard a homely story of a New York City newsboy from the slums. He was in a batch of slum boys sent into the country for two weeks by the Fresh Air Fund.

He found himself, at the end of the journey, in a large, comfortable farmhouse. A motherly woman received him cordially. When bedtime came she took him to a bedroom.

And she talked to him, as she turned down the bed covers. This had been her own son's room when he was a boy, she explained. She hoped he would enjoy a good sleep, and be down early in the morning, and so she bade him "good-night."

Morning came, and breakfast time, but the

boy didn't appear. She called up the stairs but there was no response.

She went up-stairs, found the room door open, and looked in. But there was no boy to be seen. Where was the boy?

Perplexed and wondering, her eye caught sight of a ragged shoe on the floor at the edge of the bed. Stooping down she saw the boy sound asleep on the floor under the bed.

She called to him: "Time to get up, my boy, breakfast ready." He came crawling out, rubbing his eyes, "Yes'm, yes'm."

And as she turned to leave she said quietly pointing to the bed, "Why didn't you sleep in the bed?"

The boy turned a surprised look, following the line of her pointing finger, toward the bed. "Bed!" he said simply. "Is that a bed?"

He had never slept in a bed. A door-stoop, a box, a barrel, or the like, had been the only bed the boy had ever known. Ah! yes, there are hundreds of them in the heathen slum fringe of all our great cities.

Are you sleeping under the bed, taking less than Christ has provided?

VIII

THE DEVIL'S HEALING: IMITATIONS AND COUNTERFEITS

It is Christ's first will for us that we should be pure in heart, strong in purpose, quick and accurate in discerning evil under any disguise, poised and mature in judgment, gentle in our contacts, with an inner song ringing, content in circumstances, and healed of all our bodily ills and ailments, according to His Word, through glad surrender of habit and life to His Spirit's touch.

The Devil—the Ape of God.

God is love. The Devil is hate. Love is good, the best good there can be. Hate is bad, at the worst badness.

The two are sworn enemies. The conflict is utterly irreconcilable. There can be no patched-up truce. It's an advantage to get that fact clear.

Neither side will yield. The Devil won't give in. He is incorrigible. God can't give in. His purity, His character, forbid.

The warfare goes on ceaselessly, but—not interminably. There'll be an end to it some day, a blessed end, for man.

The earth is the battlefield. Man is the one being fought for. Man's choice, freely given, is the one thing aimed at in the fighting.

God wants man's love, that is, himself at his true native best. He wants his love freely, voluntarily given. That's really repetition. Love isn't love unless it's freely given.

The Devil wants man's worship, his submission, abject, absolute submission, no matter how given or gotten. And he's dead-set on getting it.

The Devil is always on the heels of God to hurt man. Anything will be used that does that. Everything is used that promises that. Nothing is too base or foul, or too refined or cultured, for His reaching hand.

The rarest scholarship and finest culture, the foulest sensuality and most heartless selfishness, each is used to the utmost. Anything to befool and befoul, to get twists and quirks, to lead away from that touch with God which is native to man as God made him.

Nothing is too sacred for the Devil's touch. Christian phraseology, scholastic philosophy, scientific research, are laid under tribute. The sweetest relationships and purest contacts of life are foully besmirched.

And nothing is too foul if it'll help out his incorrigible purpose. And no combination of the sacred and the foul is left untried and unused.

But, *but*, God is ever on the heels of the Devil to help. That's why Christ came, and came as He came, and died as He did. Nothing God has is too precious to be freely given and sacrificed if only man may be saved from the foul touch of the Devil.

The Devil is an imitator. He's a skilled artful imitator. He never originates. But he has great ability as an imitator.

One of the early Christian leaders called the Devil "the ape of God." Imitation is the outstanding trait of both the ape and the Devil. But that was said long ago, long before the leaders' visions had become so obscured.

The Devil doesn't hesitate to deceive. He is dishonest, as well as the father of all sorts of lies. He even slanders God. He doesn't play fair.

God is so honest. He is always so fair, even, *even*, be it said plainly, to His arch-enemy. And He knows well the outcome.

The Devil is bold, devilishly bold, in his imitations and deceptions. He even imitates God! He steals phraseology from God's Book. He copies God's actions, that is, as nearly as he can.

The expert instantly detects the imitation, the counterfeit, when put side by side with the genuine. But then the experts in this line are rather few and scarce.

The one school started for teaching and training eyes and ears and judgment in this sort of thing has been skilfully turned aside from its great task.

The thing most lacking in Christian circles is teaching, simple, clear, poised teaching. Characteristically, the Christian groups are untaught and untrained.

They are like shepherdless sheep, torn, distressed, befooled, heading this way and that, and running into each other, rather violently sometimes. It's a marked feature of the spirit conflict, just now.

The great steadying factor is that the outcome is as assured as that Christ emptied that new-hewn tomb of rock, when its purpose had been served.

Miracles appeal to the imagination as nothing else does. Any evidence or suggestion of supernatural power in action attracts the biggest crowds in the shortest time. This has always been true, and is.

It has always been popularly supposed that the supernatural is God at work. A miracle is commonly taken as evidence of divine power. This is a universal common notion or delusion, and has always been so.

Of course, intelligent, thoughtful, Christian men know that this is not so. Archbishop Trench, the eminent Irish scholar and saint, speaks of this in his notable work on miracles.

A miracle is not necessarily evidence of God's work. It is evidence merely that some supernatural power is in action.

Then the questions are: whose? what? There are two sources of supernatural power, God and the Devil. Of course, God's power is absolute and limitless.

The Devil is distinctly limited. His power is actually much less than sometimes supposed. Still there is a supernatural power there, however limited. And he is very skilful in using and displaying it to the best advantage.

And we are pretty much a very unsophisticated lot. Yes, we are worse than unsophisticated. We are pretty apt to think we know, and to be rather set in thinking that way. We prefer to think so.

What a spectacle! Ignorant, and think we know! A mixture of a little knowledge, much ignorance, and more contentment with ourselves just as we are. That's the hardest kind of folk to help. That unseen fighter is surely a cunning strategist.

The Book of God gives clear light on every sort of serious question. It will answer, and answer fully, any thoughtful question brought to it.

It gives light here. It tells about satanic miracles. A miracle, you will remember, is the result of some power in action greater than men are familiar with. It does not mean something contrary to nature, but something more than the natural thing we are commonly used to.

The Devil's Miracles in Egypt.

The Book tells distinctly about the Devil's miracles. There are two groups of passages, one past, one regarding the future; Egypt in the past, and the earth-wide Crisis that is yet future.

In the case of Egypt, it is a time of partial visitation of judgment on the world-empire of its day. Moses performed ten miracles, by God's direction, that entered vitally into the very life of the nation.

The Egyptian magicians, or occult experts, performed three miracles in imitation of Moses, attempted a fourth, but failed in it,

Then, frankly, with awe-stricken faces, they admitted that there was a power at work through Moses superior to them, distinctly greater than the power they stood for.

The line of conflict here is quite sharply drawn. Moses acted by God's direction. The Egyptian king opposed him contemptuously, then stubbornly, then incorrigibly.

The magicians were the king's servants. They were the experts of that time in the occult, in dealing with unseen spirits and spirit forces. They were experts in the black art.

They were loyal to Pharaoh in his resisting and scoffing at God. They fought Moses and God, with all the power at their command.

The line of conflict could not be more clearly marked. The Devil was opposing God. God and the Devil were the real spirit opponents behind the human scenes.

The striking thing just now is that there were three miracles done by the magicians through the Devil's power. There was a fourth attempted but it failed, completely.

There is further the tacit inference of a limit in the Devil's power even in the three miracles actually performed.

The magicians caused their rods to become serpents. There was distinctly an evil supernatural power at work. Perhaps serpent activity was more easily within the Devil's range of action. Yet Moses' serpent swallows up the others! Moses understood that word spoken long after about treading upon serpents.

The turning of water into blood, and the plague of countless frogs, by the magicians, following Moses' initiative, again reveal the Devil's supernatural power at work. It is clearly a supernatural transaction in each case.

But there is a limitation. Moses' miracles suggest an overflowing supply of power. The other is less. The thing was done, yet, as though there was no flush of power at command, rather a scantiness.

The fourth attempt was a confessed failure. The experts confessed themselves helpless in the face of this display of God's power. They're clean outdone, outclassed. And a little later the magicians themselves are helpless sufferers when the plague of boils came.

The purpose of these satanic miracles is fourfold, to fight God, to discredit His messenger Moses, to deceive the Egyptians and indeed all the world (for such events would travel like wildfire), and to keep God's nation in slavery. It is clearly the Devil at work, behind Pharaoh, as an all too-willing tool.

The limits to the Devil's supernatural power are threefold. The miracles done are an imitation. There is no initiative. Each is distinctly less, much less in extent than the thing imitated. And there is a sharp line beyond which the Devil's power cannot go.

But the thing to mark just now is this: the

Devil can work miracles. He has supernatural power, with sharp definite limitation.

The Devil's Healings in the Coming Crisis.

Then we swing to the other end of the Book. There is a time of Crisis repeatedly spoken of, world-wide, preceding a New Order of Things on the earth.

It will be a time of marked satanic activity. And in connection with that there will be miracles of healing done by the Devil.

His purpose of course is to deceive, to drive through his own plans, and to tighten his hold on men's lives. Let us look at the Scripture teaching regarding this.

The common phrase in the New Testament for miracles is the phrase "signs and wonders." Sometimes the language used is "signs," sometimes "signs and wonders," sometimes "signs and wonders and powers," sometimes "signs and powers." A few times the word "miracles" is used.

Now, by far the greater number of the miracles so specified are miracles of bodily healing. Of the thirty-three miracles done by Christ twenty-four are miracles of bodily healing. And four others have to do with bodily need.

In the Book of Acts the use of this phrase for miracles of healing is yet more marked. Practically the phrase "signs and wonders," with its variations, is the equivalent in the New Testament for miracles of bodily healing. Other usage is so exceptional as to emphasize this as the common rule.

Now, the striking thing to mark is that this is the phrase used for a distinctive phase of satanic activity during that coming Crisis. There are three outstanding passages, in the Gospels, by Paul, and in the Revelation.

In that significant Olivet Talk with four disciples, within a week of the tragic end, Christ is speaking of the Crisis preceding His own Coming and the New Order of Things.

He speaks of various characteristics of that tribulation-crisis. He says "There shall arise false Christs (evil men pretending to be Christ), and false prophets (or religious teachers), and shall show *great signs and wonders;*"

And then the specific purpose of this is directly stated. It is directed against Christ's followers. It is "to lead astray, if (that be) possible, even the elect," *i. e.*, Christ's own people.[1]

Taking the phrase "signs and wonders" at its common meaning in the New Testament, this would mean, to the four disciples listening, that there will be marked miracles of healing, by satanic power, during that climax of evil, for the express purpose of deceiving and leading astray Christ's own people.

In his second letter to the disciples at Thessalonica Paul is answering some questions that have arisen about just when Christ's return was to be expected.

And he explains that there would be a great

[1] Matthew 24:24, Mark 13:22.

evil leader in action, about whom the coming Crisis will centre.

This leader would be at the very height of his blasphemous career at the time of Christ's coming. He would be destroyed by the glorious appearance of Christ (the blazing forth or shining forth of His arrival).

Then Paul speaks of the marked traits of this strange, foul, evil leader, the Antichrist, this personification of the Devil. His activity will be "according to the working of Satan with all *power and signs and wonders of falsehood*," or "lying wonders."

That is, these miracles are done, in imitation of Christ's miracles, to deceive the people and lead them astray.[1]

Here is this same phrase again. Paul's use of it would mean only one thing to these Thessalonian disciples, and that is, miracles of healing, by satanic power, to deceive.

There is a parallel passage to this in one of Moses' talks in the Plains of Moab.[2] He is speaking of what is to be done in case a false prophet certified his message by "a sign or a wonder," and the miraculous thing actually taking place, so as to lead the people away from the true worship. Plainly the thing was quite familiar to these people.

John's Patmos Revelation message has the same thing. It is spoken of repeatedly as one of the marked characteristics of the campaign of deception in that brief terrific future Crisis.

[1] 2 Thessalonians 2:9, 10.   [2] Deuteronomy 13:1-3.

The Devil's Healing

There's a description of the activity of a leader of evil who will be the immediate associate of that foul Antichrist.[1] He is a religious leader, a sort of court-preacher to the Antichrist himself who reigns as a king of kings for a brief time.

Among other things in the description this stands out, "and he doeth *great signs* that he should even make fire to come down out of heaven upon the earth in the sight of men. And he deceiveth them that dwell on the earth by reason of *the signs* ——"

The startling thing of fire coming down is specified in speaking of the great signs. This is particularized because it is something unusual, in addition to the usual meaning of the phrase "great signs."

A little later John is told of happenings toward the end of that troublous crisis period. There will be sent out by the Devil himself and by his two chief leaders, the Antichrist and his court-preacher, "spirits of demons *working signs,*" sent into all the earth.[2]

And in speaking of the utter defeat and rout of the Antichrist and his evil associates, this court-preacher who is spoken of here as the false religious teacher, is identified as the one "that wrought the signs . . . wherewith he deceived them ——" Clearly these *signs* are an outstanding feature.[3] This emphasis of a five-fold repetition is striking.

[1] Revelation 13: 13-14. [2] Revelation 16: 13-14.
[3] Revelation 19: 19, 20.

About the Healing Christ

The whole New Testament use of the phrase makes clear that miracles of healing by satanic power will be one of the commonest, if not the most common, feature of that crisis time that is coming, some time.

And the whole purpose in this is to deceive the people, and particularly the Church constituency. It is to make them think that it is God at work.

And, uninstructed as they so largely are, and so not keen to discern, they will be easy prey to these tactics.

The Devil's Healing To-day.

But one need not go back to Egypt, nor forward to the coming crisis time. He can find references closer at hand in the Book of Life, being written daily. Our own time is witnessing this sort of thing in marked measure, and increasing extent.

The Church of Christ has not been true to the full Gospel of Christ. I say that very thoughtfully and sadly. I do not say it to criticise the Church, but only to help understand things at the present time a bit better.

I love the Church. I reverence its past, and its present inestimable service in the world. If my words seem critical, I am simply criticising myself, so far as any man is a part of the Church.

With fine exceptions, the Church of Christ has not told out fully in any generation, since the first few Christian centuries, the full rounded Gospel of Christ.

And so it is not a surprising thing that there have grown up false teachings, and false systems of teaching, about bodily healing.

The very need, sore need, of the crowds everywhere in this regard has made a rare opportunity to teach about bodily healing in a wrong way.

The people are hungry, eager for help. And the Devil has never been known to be slow in using every door open to him, or that he could pry open.

Just now there is a system of teaching about healing, and a system of healing, that holds the centre of the stage.

It has grown up within living memory, and within the past ten years seems to have grown more vigorous than ever.

It has spread like a cursed wildfire in our own land, up and down Europe, into the African edges, and the Orient, and indeed wherever the Anglo-American trail leaves traces.

It uses Christ's name quite freely. It quotes or rather half-quotes, misquotes, the Bible. Its teaching is a mixture of Christian phraseology, devout language, psychological half-truths, and positive untruths.

It makes pretense of being a Christian Church. I need not repeat its name, it is so well known. And the thing to mark just now is that people are healed through its ministrations, within sharply marked limitations and restrictions.

There's no question that people do experience, through its teaching, healing of a certain sort, up to a certain extent. That fact is quite clear.

It will be remembered what has been said in a previous Talk on the seven ways in which healing comes to one's body.[1]

The Creator has graciously put a healing power within the human body. There is natural healing without conscious coöperation on our part.

There is this same natural healing assisted by an intelligent understanding and coöperation. An enlightened instructed understanding of this remarkable healing power in the body, and our intelligent coöperation, make an enormous difference. It helps greatly.

Our mental attitude is often the decisive thing in illness, turning the tide in favour of healing and health. This is spoken of somewhat fully in the previous Talk referred to.

This is the second way in which healing comes. It should be noted. It will be spoken of again later.

Then there is healing through this same natural power assisted by human wisdom and skill, both personal and professional.

Still further, there is healing sometimes through this natural power in our bodies *overcoming* what may have been done by blundering unwise human touch. These are the four natural ways.

[1] See chapter "How Does Christ Heal?"

There are two supernatural ways. There is healing by Christ's direct touch, a supernatural touch, in addition to the creative natural power spoken of. And, of course, this little series of "Quiet Talks" is devoted to that one thing.

Then there is a healing by *the Devil's touch,* a supernatural touch. And there may be a blending of two or more of these.

Seven ways in which healing may come to one's body, four natural, two supernatural, and one a blend or combination of two or more of these.

Now, it should be keenly noted, that in this false system we are talking about, this so-called Christian system, the healings that do occur come through two of these ways.

There is much emphasis put on the second of these, the human understanding of, and cooperating with, that natural healing power.

I do not mean to say that it is taught in a clear, intelligent fashion. Clear teaching is conspicuously absent here. It is quite doubtful if the thing is intelligently understood so as to give clear teaching.

There is a strange garbled mixture of truths and half-truths and positive not-truths. But through all there is a continual emphasis on one's mental attitude.

And so far as this insistence actually affects one's attitude that inner power of healing swings into action. And this, be it noted, is good so far as it is good.

If the teaching were clear, and more, if it

were put in right connection with other teaching that belongs with it, the results would be yet better. But, of course, nothing of that good sort could be gotten here.

There is no evil system of teaching all bad. It would fall of its own dead weight. The Devil always steals a veneering of some truth for his lies. He is the first expert in the fine art of camouflage.

The truth about the influence of the mind on the body, so little appreciated to the full by any one, was true for Adam and Eve in Eden, for Cain outside Eden, with the wickedest man that ever lived as with the saintliest, in savage wilds as in cultured centres.

God's creative touch is never off any man's body. This is one of the seven ways of healing emphasized partly by this false system of healing.

There is a second way used in this false teaching. It brings in a strange fact, that makes one stare out. *The Devil heals* through this so-called Christian teaching. The evidence is clear, and the fact indisputable.

"Why," you instantly cry out, "the Devil heal! Absurd! Ridiculous! The Devil is bad. Healing is only good. Will a bad Devil do a good thing?"

And the answer to that is quite clear and positive. A bad Devil will do a good thing for a bad purpose, to get hold on a man's life, and to tighten his hold.

A mongrel cur back of your dwelling disturbs

your night's sleep, night after night. You are too gentle-hearted perhaps to use a revolver.

So you get a bit of good meat and some bad poison. You combine them dexterously. You throw the mixture in the back alley.

The dog has no sense of discernment between good meat and bad poison. He eats the good meat greedily. He gets the bad poison.

The city's garbage cart has an extra job. And now your night's slumbers are undisturbed. The strategy was a success.

Some dear good people, even some saintly Christian folk, might claim close kinship with that dog in one particular. They have no discernment, no spirit discernment.

They are easily caught with the Christian phraseology in the false teaching, but don't detect the absence of the real thing, the actual presence of the Devil's own teachings.

Christ's Blood the Touchstone.

Spirit discernment is one of the rarest, if not the rarest thing to-day. This is true even in cultured Christian circles. It is strangely true how strangely lacking discernment is.

The outstanding characteristic of preaching to-day is the bewitching, bewildering mixture and blend of half-truths, positive non-truths, and utter absence of the really few essential truths.

The whole is covered with a more or less highly polished veneering of either religious talk or Christian verbiage. And the pleasing personality, vigorous mentality, fine diction, scholarly quotations and allusions, all this befogs as to the real message being given.

This is true of all communions, and in all parts of Christendom, and into the mission lands, with fine exceptions.

But how shall we common folk know what teaching to accept about bodily healing? We are all busy earning bread and drink, boots and income tax. We can't all be experts. How shall we know?

And the answer is simple. A single ray of clear shining of the sun will pierce clear through the pretty French-gray fogs that gather.

There is a touchstone by which to test any teaching whether in type or on tongue. It's an acid test, unfailing.

And this is the test: the distinctive singular personality of Christ, and the distinctive solitary meaning of His death on Calvary and His living again afterward.

There is no blood-red tinge to the false teachings spoken of. It is never safe to accept supernatural healing except where the deity of Christ is distinctly emphasized, and the sacrificial blood He shed for us, as none other did nor could nor can, is made blessedly prominent.

The Devil hates the blood of the solitary God-Man. He fears it. He crouches terrified, and flees where it is emphasized and pled in prayer. It, *it*, the blood, spells out his stinging defeat. And right well he knows it.

Under all this vague verbiage, this befogging

The Devil's Healing

talk about the inspiration of the Book, and the virgin birth, and the tremendous event of the third-morning-after, lies the distinct Devil touch and trail, and hate and dread.

The healing that, without question, comes in connection with this false so-called Christian teaching has this twofold source.

It comes through the working of that natural healing and the right mental attitude of which we have commonly been taught so little.

God is always true to His truth, and to Himself, and to us men, even though the Devil himself seek to pervert things.

And further there is no question that *the Devil heals*, so far as he can, through this false so-called Christian teaching.

But two things should be keenly noted about the Devil's healing. There is a distinct line beyond which he cannot go. Over that line he is powerless.

Christ healed perfectly and permanently and instantly, and He still does when we allow it. The Devil's healings are never perfect nor permanent.

One remembers the Egyptian story. There the Devil's supernatural power was limited, sharply limited, and indeed within narrow limits. In comparison with God it was scanty, as though with an effort, and with a small result. And it was in imitation always, mere imitation.

The second thing to mark yet more sharply is this. *The Devil's healing makes slaves.* It is a striking thing, of which the instances are countless, that the healing that comes through the Devil's imitation of Christ leads to a servile degrading bondage.

There is a bondage of spirit, of mental vigour, and a moral bondage that has a vise-like grip. One stumbles constantly over these mental, moral wrecks.

That slavery can be broken only through the power of the blood of Christ, and then usually only through the severest mental and spirit struggle. But it can be broken. Christ, Christ's blood, will set any one blessedly free.

Any one, any time, who will, may come to Christ, trusting as simply as a little child and as fully as the maturest man.

With all his perplexities and burdens he may come. And Christ never fails. His blood cleanseth from sin. It breaks the Devil's shackles. And it heals our bodies.

Observations for fully a quarter of a century, in many lands, with all sorts of persons, with countless interviews, confirms by personal knowledge what is being said. The Book of Life has furnished illustrations for all these statements.

The Power of the Blood of Christ.

One winter my wife and I met a German head-deaconess in Stockholm, and learned from her lips an unusual incident.

She was a woman in middle life, of large frame and full of physical vigour. She was engaged, and had been for years, in mission work in Berlin, especially among girls and young women who had been led astray.

We were guests together in the same home for a week, and had many opportunities for fellowship and exchange of experiences.

We came to respect her for her homely common sense, and cautious mature judgments, and to love her for her evident saintliness and her sacrificial life in the difficult field of service into which she had been led.

The incident I am speaking of now was one of many. I would hesitate to tell it were it not for the sanity, and cautiousness, and thoughtful care in detailed observation, that marked the deaconess' speech.

But as I listened and questioned and thought and prayed throughout that week, I found an answer of acceptance in my inner spirit to her unusual story.

The story was of a woman whom the deaconess knew personally. This woman lived out in the country not far from Berlin. Her little daughter accidentally fell into an open fire, and was seriously burned in her face.

The woman did a thing that seems incredible. And yet the more one comes in touch with actual life in the old world the less incredible it seems. Facts open one's eyes.

The woman said that she went out to an old tree in the forest, and there made a compact with the Devil that if he would heal her daughter of the burn she would serve him faithfully.

The thing seemed impossible, both in the willingness to do such a thing, and that such a transaction could take place.

But the woman herself afterward told the story to the deaconess who was telling us. And it was clearly real to the woman who said she made the pact.

The woman said that at once her child's face was as if the fire had not touched it. The healing seemed complete. No scars remained. That's the first part of the story.

The child grew to be a young woman of fine sweet beauty of face and form. Meanwhile they had moved in to Berlin and settled there.

The young woman attended some meetings at a mission hall and was deeply impressed. And one night she accepted Christ as her personal Saviour, and dedicated her life to Him. I think the mother herself had become a Christian about this same time.

And, at once, the marks of the fire appeared on her daughter's face as though just fresh. The deaconess was present. They were all greatly distressed. The mother explained to the deaconess about the earlier experience.

The deaconess knew about Christ's healing power, and so taught them. They had a time of prayer together. And again, the deaconess told us, the healing touch, Christ's healing touch, came. And again the young woman's face showed no marks of the fire. The deaconess herself witnessed this.

That was the deaconess' story. The thing seemed quite incredible. But we were in the home for a week with this thoughtful, matured, rarely-poised, saintly woman.

And as the days passed, and I studied her, and talked with her from day to day, and questioned, the conviction deepened that she was reliable.

Her caution, her detail of description, her habitual accuracy of observation, and her carefulness in statement, quite convinced me of her reliability as a witness of what she told us. And so I have repeated her story here.

The story is the more striking in telling of a double healing, the Devil's and Christ's. There is the rivalry very real between the two, bitter and hopeless on the Devil's side; insistent and certain of victory on Christ's side.

And the human will, sovereign in its choice, decides in that conflict. Here was a decisive defeat for the Devil, and the sweeping victory of Christ, on the battlefield of one human life. And the young woman's decision, insisted on under sore stress, was the decisive thing.

The Devil's intense selfishness stands out, his spite spirit. He touches only to hurt. He helps only to help himself. He helps only to hurt.

The Devil is all for himself. There was the ugly fling-back of a defeated foe. He would do his worst when forced to go.

The Devil is always on the heels of God to hurt. God is ever quick as a flash on the heels of the Devil to reach eagerly out and help and heal.

Christ was God Himself coming down to the battlefield. He gave the Devil the decisive blow.

And so man may be set quite free. And so he is made strong to choose right, and only right, regardless of consequences.

The School of Discernment.

The great need to-day among Christian people is *spirit discernment*. Please note: not the critical spirit that hunts heresies and picks flaws.

That only hurts the hunter and helps no one. Nagging criticism is like a sharp-edged knife that has no hilt. It cuts the hand that uses it, and cuts deep.

Discernment means the trained ear that listens attentively, and discerns the main thing being taught, under whatever rhetorical veneering.

It means the opened eye quick to see between the lines what is really there, maybe in hiding.

It means the humble spirit, willing to see its own faults and defects, only eager to be right. It means the loving spirit quick to give any help to any man.

The sore need to-day is for teaching, not argument and discussion, but teaching. Never was the need sorer. Argument only hardens. Each side is more set. And the crowd cheers or jeers, according to their preconceived preferences.

Teaching, the clear, positive, patient teaching of God's truth, put into the sort of language men think in, with homely illustrations out of real life, this is sorely needed.

One should set himself to cultivate an accurate discernment or appraisal of all that meets his eye and ear. He should do it for self-protection, and for true culture, and to help others.

There's a School of Discernment. One may well take time for a special course. The requirements for entrance are few and simple. They are five in number, an act, a habit, a book, a bit of time, and a spirit.

The act? surrender to Christ as the Master. The habit? doing habitually what would please Him in everything. And when in doubt, *don't*.

The Book? this rare, singularly, solitary Book of God. The time? the daily bit of quiet time off alone with the Book, with the mind alert, and the spirit open.

The spirit? the spirit of prayer for understanding, discernment, seeing things as they are. And with this goes the thoughtful, brooding spirit.

And with all of these goes the willing spirit, willingness to accept facts and conclusions that you don't like, that run crosswise to your preconceptions and preferences and habits.

If we will only start in this school, and attend faithfully it will be of the rarest value in the coming days, the coming difficult days.

The outcome will be mental and spirit discernment, a keen, a growing discernment. And with it will go the brotherly spirit that will help any one in personal need no matter how he differs with you, or criticises you.

He that is willing to do Christ's will for him, regardless of how it may change some personal things, will have in increasing degree that keen, clear knowledge of truth, of the Book's teaching, of Christ Himself who embodies all truth in Himself.[1]

The clear vision, the discriminating ear, the balanced understanding of things that differ, the obedient spirit, the heart of love in all one's personal contacts, these are some results of attendance at the Discernment School.

But whether in school or out, the outstanding thing just now is this. There's healing for our bodies through the solitary God-Man who died as none other did nor could nor can, and lived again, and still lives.

And through this Man's blood there's deliverance from any bondage that has come, full, sweet, glad, free deliverance.

And Christ waits at your side now.

[1] John 7:17.

Printed in the United States
144670LV00003BA/55/A